TABLE OF CONTENTS

Top 20 Test Taking Tips

1. Carefully follow all the test registration procedures
2. Know the test directions, duration, topics, question types, how many questions
3. Setup a flexible study schedule at least 3-4 weeks before test day
4. Study during the time of day you are most alert, relaxed, and stress free
5. Maximize your learning style; visual learner use visual study aids, auditory learner use auditory study aids
6. Focus on your weakest knowledge base
7. Find a study partner to review with and help clarify questions
8. Practice, practice, practice
9. Get a good night's sleep; don't try to cram the night before the test
10. Eat a well balanced meal
11. Know the exact physical location of the testing site; drive the route to the site prior to test day
12. Bring a set of ear plugs; the testing center could be noisy
13. Wear comfortable, loose fitting, layered clothing to the testing center; prepare for it to be either cold or hot during the test
14. Bring at least 2 current forms of ID to the testing center
15. Arrive to the test early; be prepared to wait and be patient
16. Eliminate the obviously wrong answer choices, then guess the first remaining choice
17. Pace yourself; don't rush, but keep working and move on if you get stuck
18. Maintain a positive attitude even if the test is going poorly
19. Keep your first answer unless you are positive it is wrong
20. Check your work, don't make a careless mistake

Early Childhood Development

Sensorimotor period of cognitive development

From birth to 1 month old, infants learn to comprehend their environment through their inborn reflexes, such as the sucking reflex and the reflex of looking at their surroundings. From 1–4 months old, babies begin to coordinate their physical sensations with new schemas, i.e. mental constructs/concepts they form to represent elements of reality. For example, an infant might suck her thumb by chance and feel pleasure from the activity; in the future, she will repeat thumb-sucking because the pleasure is rewarding. Piaget called this second substage "Primary Circular Reactions." In the third substage, around 4–8 months, which he called "Secondary Circular Reactions," children also repeat rewarding actions, but now they are focused on things in the environment that they can affect, rather than just the child's own person. For example, once a baby learns to pick up an object and mouth it, s/he will repeat this. Thus, babies learn an early method of environmental exploration through their mouths, an extension of their initial sucking reflex.

According to Piaget, babies about 8–12 months are in the "Coordination of Reactions" substage of the Sensorimotor stage. Having begun repeating actions purposely to achieve environmental effects during the previous substage of Secondary Circular Reactions, in Coordination of Reactions, infants begin further exploring their surroundings. They frequently imitate others' observed behaviors. They more obviously demonstrate intentional behaviors. They become able to combine schemas (mental constructs) to attain certain results. They develop object permanence, the understanding that unseen objects still exist. They learn to associate certain objects with their properties. For example, once a baby realizes a rattle makes a noise when shaken, s/he will deliberately shake it to produce the sound. In "Tertiary Circular Reactions," at about 12–18 months, children begin experimenting through trial-and-error. For instance, a child might test various actions or sounds for getting parents' attention. From 18–24 months, in the substage of "Early Representational Thought," children begin representing objects and events with symbols. They begin to understand the world via not only actions, but mental operations.

From birth until about 2 years of age, infants are in what Piaget termed the Sensorimotor stage of cognitive development. They learn through environmental input they receive through their senses; motor actions they engage in; and through feedback they receive from their bodies and the environment about their actions. For example, a baby kicks his legs, sees his feet moving, and reaches for them. He sees objects, reaches for them, and grasps them. Eventually, babies learn they can make some objects move by touching or hitting them. They learn through repeated experiences that when they throw objects out of their cribs, their parents retrieve them. They will seem to make a game of this, not to annoy parents, but as a way of learning rules of cause and effect by repeating actions to see the same results. They also enjoy their ability to be causal agents and their power to achieve effects through their actions.

Object permanence

One of the landmarks of infant cognitive development is learning that concrete objects are not "out of sight, out of mind"; in other words, things still continue to exist even when they are out of our sight. Babies generally develop this realization around 8–9 months old, though some may be earlier or later. Some researchers after Piaget have found object permanence in babies as young as 3½ months. Younger infants typically attend to an object of interest only when they can see it; if it is removed or hidden, they are upset/confused at its disappearance and/or shift their attention to something else. A sign that they have developed object permanence is if they search for the object after it is moved or hidden. Babies only become interested in "hide and seek" types of games once they have developed this understanding that the existence of objects and people persist beyond their immediate vision or proximity. Another example of emerging object permanence is the delight babies begin to take in "peek-a-boo" games.

Schema

Piaget proposed we form mental constructs or concepts that he called schemata, representing elements of the environment, beginning in infancy. A schema does not represent an individual object, but a category or class of things. For example, a baby might form a schema representing "things to suck on," initially including her bottle, her thumb, and her pacifier. Piaget said assimilation is when we can fit something new into an existing schema: the child in this example assimilates "Daddy's knee" into her schema of things she can suck on when she discovers this action. When something new cannot be assimilated into an existing schema, we either modify that schema or form a new schema, which both constitute accommodation. The baby in our example, becoming a toddler, might modify her schema of things to suck to include straws, which require a different sucking technique. Piaget said assimilation and accommodation combined constitute the process of adaptation, i.e. adjusting, to our environment through interacting with it.

A toddler on an airplane sees a nearby stranger who is male, about 5'8", with white hair and eyeglasses. Both of his grandfathers have these same general appearances. He murmurs to himself, "Hi, Granddaddy."

The toddler in this example did not actually mistake a complete stranger for either one of his grandfathers. Notice that he did not directly address the stranger as "Granddaddy" with conversational loudness, but murmured it to himself. He recognized this man was not someone he knew. However, he recognized common elements with his grandfathers in the man's appearance. According to Piaget's theory of cognitive development, the explanation for this is that the child had formed a schema, i.e. a mental construct, to represent men about 5'8" with white hair and eyeglasses, based initially on his early knowledge of two such men he knew, his grandfathers, and then extending to include other similar-appearing men, through the process of assimilation of new information into an existing schema. His description did not mean he thought the stranger was named "Granddaddy." Rather, the word "Granddaddy" was not only the name he called one grandfather, but also the word he used to label his schema for all men who appeared to fit into this category.

A toddler sees a large, brown dog through the window and says, "Moo."

Piaget found that forming schemas, or mental constructs to represent objects and actions, is how babies and children learn about themselves and the world through their interactions with their bodies and the environment. If they can fit a new experience into an existing schema, they assimilate it; or when necessary, they change an existing schema or form a new one to accommodate a new stimulus. Therefore, in this example, the toddler had seen cows in picture books, photos, or on a farm, and learned to associate the sound "Moo" with

- 6 -

cows, reinforced by the teaching of toys, books, and adults. She had formed a schema for large, brown, four-legged, furry animals. Because the dog she saw fit these properties, she assimilated the dog into her cow schema. If she were then told this was a dog that says "Bow-wow," she would either form a new schema for dogs; or, if she had previously only seen smaller dogs, accommodate (modify) her existing dog schema to include larger dogs.

Conservation

Conservation is the cognitive ability to understand that objects or substances retain their properties of numbers or amounts even when their appearance, shape, or configuration changes. Piaget found from his experiments with children that this ability develops around the age of five years. He also found children develop conservation of number, length, mass, weight, volume, and quantity respectively at slightly different ages. One example of a conservation experiment is with liquid volume: the experimenter pours the same amount of liquid into a short, wide container and a tall, thin one. Children who have not developed conservation of liquid volume typically say one container has more liquid, even though they saw both amounts were equal, based on one container's looking fuller. Similarly, children who have not developed conservation of number, shown equal numbers of beads, usually say a group arranged in a long row has more beads than a group clustered together. Children having developed conservation recognize the amounts are the same regardless of appearance.

Piaget

Piaget's Preoperational stage of cognitive development
Children between (roughly) two and six years old are in Piaget's Preoperational stage of cognitive development. Having begun to use objects to represent other things, i.e. symbolic representation, near the end of the previous Sensorimotor stage, children now further develop this ability during pretend/make-believe play. They may pretend a broom is a guitar or a horse; or talk using a block as a phone. Toddlers begin to play "house," pretending they and their playmates are the mommy, the daddy, the mailman, the doctor, etc. The reason Piaget called this stage Preoperational is that children are not yet capable of performing mental "operations," including following concrete logic or manipulating information mentally. Their thinking is intuitive rather than following logical steps. Piaget termed Preoperational children "egocentric" in that they literally cannot adopt another's point of view, even concretely: in experiments, after seeing pictures of a scene as viewed from different positions, children could not match a picture to another person's position, selecting the picture showing the scene from their own viewpoint.

Piaget's Preoperational vs. Concrete Operational stages of cognitive development
The different thinking found between Piaget's Preoperational and Concrete Operations stages is exemplified in experiments he and others conducted to prove his theory. For example, the absence/presence of ability to conserve liquid volume across shape/appearance has been shown in experiments with differently aged children. A preschooler is shown a tall, thin beaker and a short, wide one. The experimenter also shows the child two identically sized and shaped containers with identical amounts of liquid in each. The experimenter then pours the equal amounts of liquid into the two differently shaped beakers. The preschooler will say either the thin beaker holds more liquid because it is taller or the short beaker holds more because it is wider. Piaget termed this "centration"—focusing on only one property at a time. An older child "decentrates," can

- 7 -

"conserve" the amount, and knows both beakers hold identical amounts. Older children also use reversibility and logic, e.g. "I know they are still equal, because I just saw you pour the same amount into each beaker."

Piaget called the stage of most children aged 2–6 years Preoperational because children these ages cannot yet perform mental operations, i.e. manipulate information mentally. At around 6–7 years old, children begin to develop Concrete Operations. A key aspect of this stage is the ability to think logically. This ability first develops relative to concrete objects and events. Concrete Operational children still have trouble understanding abstract concepts or hypothetical situations, but they can apply logical sequences and cause and effect to things they can see, feel, and manipulate physically. For example, Concrete Operational children develop the understanding that things have the same amount or number regardless of their shape or arrangement, which Piaget termed conservation. They develop proficiency in inductive logic, i.e. drawing generalizations from specific instances. However, deductive logic, i.e. predicting specific results according to general principles, is not as well-developed until the later stage of Formal Operations involving abstract thought. Another key development of Concrete Operations is reversibility, i.e. the ability to reverse an action or operation.

Animism and magical thinking

Piaget found that children in the Preoperational stage are not yet able to perform logical mental operations. Their thinking is intuitive during the toddler and preschool years. One characteristic of the thinking of young children is animism, or assigning human qualities, feelings, and actions to inanimate objects. For example, a child seeing an autumn leaf fall off of a tree might remark, "The tree didn't like that leaf and pushed it off of its branch." Or a child with a sunburn might say, "The sun was angry at me and burned me." A related characteristic is magical thinking, which is attributing cause and effect relationships between their own feelings and thoughts and environmental events where none exists. For example, if a child says "I hate you" to another person or secretly dislikes and wishes the other gone, and something bad then happens to that person, the child is likely to believe what s/he said/felt/thought caused the other's unfortunate event. This is related to egocentrism—seeing everything as revolving around oneself.

Sensory, concrete, and centration characteristics of cognitive development

Preschool children do not think in the same ways as older children and adults do, as Piaget observed. Their thinking is strongly based upon and connected to their sensory perceptions. This means that in solving problems, they depend mainly on how things look, sound, feel, smell, and taste. Therefore, preschool children should always be given concrete objects that they can touch, explore, and experiment with in any learning experience. They are not yet capable of understanding abstract concepts or manipulating information mentally, so they must have real things to work with to understand premath concepts. For example, they will learn to count solid objects like blocks, beads, or pennies before they can count numbers in their heads. They cannot benefit from rote math memorization, or "sit still and listen" lessons. Since young children "centrate" on one characteristic/object/person/event at a time, adults can offer activities encouraging decentration/incorporating multiple aspects, e.g. not only grouping all triangles, but grouping all red triangles separately from blue triangles.

Stages of growth and development in art

Austrian and German art scholars established six stages in art. (1) The Scribble stage: from 2–4 years, children first make uncontrolled scribbles; then controlled scribbling; then progress to naming their scribbles to indicate what they represent. (2) The Preschematic stage: from ages 4–6, children begin to develop a visual schema. Schema, meaning mental representation, comes from Piaget's cognitive-developmental theory. Without complete comprehension of dimensions and sizes, children may draw people and houses the same height; they use color more emotionally than logically. They may omit or exaggerate facial features, or they might draw sizes by importance, e.g. drawing themselves as largest among people or drawing the most important feature, e.g. the head, as the largest or only body part. (3) The Schematic stage: from 7–9 years, drawings more reflect actual physical proportions and colors. (4) Dawning Realism: from ages 9-11, drawings become increasingly representational. (5) Children aged 11–13 are in the Pseudorealistic stage, reflecting their ability to reason. (6) Children 14+ are in the Period of Decision stage, reflecting the adolescent identity crisis.

Viktor Lowenfeld

Viktor Lowenfeld (1903–1960) taught art to elementary school students and sculpture to blind students. Lowenfeld's acquaintance with Sigmund Freud, who was interested in his work with the blind, motivated Lowenfeld to pursue scientific research. He published several books on using creative arts activities therapeutically. Lowenfeld was familiar with six stages previously identified in the growth of art. He combined these with principles of human development drawn from the school of psychoanalytic psychology founded by Freud. In his adaptation, he named the six stages reflecting the development of children's art as Scribble, Preschematic, Schematic, Dawning Realism, Pseudorealistic, and Period of Decision. Lowenfeld identified adolescent learning styles as haptic, focused on physical sensations and subjective emotional experiences, and as visual, focused on appearances, each demanding corresponding instructional approaches. Lowenfeld's book Creative and Mental Growth (1947) was the most influential text in art education during the later 20th century. Lowenfeld's psychological emphasis in this text gave scientific foundations to creative and artistic expression, and identified developmentally age-appropriate art media and activities.

Music

Development of infants and young children
Long before they can speak, and before they even comprehend much speech, infants respond to the sounds of voices and to music. These responses are not only to auditory stimulation, but moreover to the emotional content in what they hear. Parents sing lullabies to babies; not only are these sounds pleasant and soothing, but they also help children develop trust in their environment as secure. Parents communicate their love to children through singing and introduce them to experiences of pleasure and excitement through music. As children grow, music progresses to be not only a medium of communication but also one of self-expression as they learn to sing/play musical sounds. Music facilitates memory, as we see through commercial jingles and mnemonic devices. Experiments find music improves spatial reasoning. Children's learning of perceptual and logical concepts like beginning/ending, sequences, cause-and-effect, balance, harmony/dissonance and mathematical number and timing concepts is reinforced by music. Music also promotes

- 9 -

language development. Children learn about colors, counting, conceptual relationships, nature, and social skills through music.

Musical activities enhance emotional, social, aesthetic, and school readiness skills
Young children who are just learning to use spoken language often cannot express their emotions very well verbally. Music is a great aid to emotional development in that younger children can express happiness, sadness, anger, etc., through singing and/or playing music more easily than they can with words. Children of preschool ages not only listen to music and respond to what they hear, they also learn to create music through singing and playing instruments together with other children. These activities help them learn crucial social skills for their lives, like cooperating with others, collaborating, and making group or team efforts to accomplish something. When children are given guided musical experiences, they learn to make their own judgments of what is good or bad music; this provides them with the foundations for developing an aesthetic sense. Music promotes preliteracy skills by enhancing phonemic awareness. As growing children develop musical appreciation and skills, these develop fundamental motor, cognitive, and social skills they need for language, school readiness, literacy, and life.

Learning activities that help young children develop cognitive abilities

As shown by Piaget, young children have difficulty reversing operations. Adults can ask them to build block structures, for example, and then dismantle them one block at a time to reverse the construction. They can ask children to retell rhymes or stories backward. They can take small groups of children for walks and ask them if they can return by the same route as they came. Young children often assume causal relationships where none exist. Adults can provide activities to produce and observe results, e.g. pouring water into different containers; knocking over bowling pins by swinging a pendulum; rolling wheeled toys down ramps; or blowing balls through mazes, and then asking them, "What happened when you did this? What would happen if you did this? What could you do to make this happen?" Young children are also often egocentric, seeing everything from their own viewpoint. Adults can help them take others' perspectives through guessing games wherein they must give each other clues to guess persons/objects and dramatic role-playing activities, where they pretend to be others.

Physical development and brain growth

Early childhood physical growth, while significant, is slower than infant growth. From birth to 2 years, children generally grow to four times their newborn weight and 2/3 their newborn length/height. From 2–3 years, however, children usually gain only about 4 lbs. and 3.5 inches. From 4–6 years, growth slows more; gains of 5–7 lbs. and 2.5 inches are typical. Due to slowing growth rates, 3- and 4-year-olds appear to eat less food, but do not; they actually just eat fewer calories per pound of body weight. Brain growth is still rapid in preschoolers: brains attain 55 percent of adult size by 2 years, and 90 percent by 6 years. The majority of brain growth is usually by 4–4.5 years, with a growth spurt around 2 years and growth rates slowing significantly between 5 and 6 years. Larger brain size indicates not more neurons, but larger sizes; differences in their organization; more glial cells nourishing and supporting neurons; and greater myelination (development of the sheath protecting nerve fibers and facilitating their efficient intercommunication).

Gender differences in motor development

On average, preschool boys have larger muscles than preschool girls, so they can run faster, climb higher, and jump farther. Boys at these ages tend to be more muscular physically. Preschool girls, while less muscular, are on the average more mature physically for their ages than boys. While boys usually exceed girls in their large-muscle, gross-motor abilities like running, jumping, and climbing, girls tend to surpass boys in small-muscle, fine-motor abilities like buttoning buttons, using scissors, and similar activities involving the manipulation of small tools, utensils, and objects. While preschool boys exhibit more strength in large-muscle, gross-motor actions, preschool girls are more advanced than preschool boys in large-muscle, gross-motor skills that do not demand strength so much as coordination, like hopping, balancing on one foot, and skipping. While these specific gender differences in preschoolers' physical and motor development have been observed consistently in research, it is also found that preschool girls' and boys' physical and motor development patterns are generally more similar than different overall.

Abilities in perceptual development that occur in infancy

In normal development, babies have usually established the ability to see, hear, smell, taste, and feel and also the ability to integrate such sensory information by the age of six months. Additional perceptual abilities, which are less obvious and more complex, continue to emerge throughout the early childhood years. For instance, young children develop increasing precision in recognizing visual concepts like size and shape. This development allows children to identify accurately the shape and size of an object no matter from what angle they perceive it. Infants have these capacities in place, but have not yet developed accuracy in using them. For example, a baby might realize that objects farther away occupy less of their visual fields than nearer objects; however, the baby has yet to learn just how much less of the visual field is taken up by the farther object. Young children attain this and similar kinds of learning by actively, energetically exploring their environments. Such activity is crucial for developing accurate perception of size, shape, and distance.

Progress in the typical motor development of young children

Genetics, physiological maturation, nutrition, and experience through practice combine to further preschoolers' motor skills development. Newborns' reflexive behaviors progress to preschoolers' voluntary activities. Also, children's perception of the size, shape, and position of the body and body parts becomes more accurate by preschool ages. In addition, increases in bilateral coordination of the body's two sides enhance preschoolers' motor skills. Motor skills development entails both learning new movements and gradually integrating previously learned movements into smooth, continuous patterns, as in learning to throw a ball with skill. Both large muscles, for gross-motor skills like climbing, running, and jumping, and small muscles, for fine-motor skills like drawing and tying knots, develop. Eye-hand coordination involves fine-motor control. Preschoolers use visual feedback, i.e. seeing whether they are making things go where and do what they want them to, in learning to manipulate small objects with their hands and fingers.

Nature-nurture interaction

The physical development of babies and young children is a product of the interactions between genetic and environmental factors. Also, a child's physical progress is equally influenced by environmental and psychological variables. For the body, brain, and nervous system to grow and develop normally, children must live in healthy environments. When the interaction of hereditary and environmental influences is not healthful, this is frequently reflected in abnormal patterns of growth. Failure to thrive syndrome is a dramatic example. When children are abused or neglected for long periods of time, they actually stop growing. The social environments of such children create psychological stress. This stress makes the child's pituitary gland stop releasing growth hormones, and growth ceases. When such environmental stress is relieved and these children are given proper care, stimulation, and affection, they begin growing again. They often grow rapidly enough to catch up on the growth they missed earlier. Normal body and brain growth—as well as psychological development—depend upon the collaboration of nature and nurture.

Interpreting pictures and eye movements

As adults, our ability to look at pictures of people and things in the environment is something we usually take for granted. Researchers have established that 3-year-old children's responses indicate their ability to recognize shading, line convergence, and other cues of depth in two-dimensional pictures. However, scientists have also found that children's sensitivity to these kinds of visual cues increases as they grow older. The eye movements and eye fixation patterns of young children affect their ability to get the most complete and accurate information from pictorial representations of reality. When viewing pictures, adults sweep the entire picture to see it as a whole, their eye movements leaping around; to focus on specific details, adults use shorter eye movements. Preschool children differ from adults in using shorter eye movements overall, and focusing on small parts of the picture near the center or an edge. They therefore disregard, or do not see, a lot of the picture's available information.

Characteristics in art that reflects perceptual, cognitive, and motor development

Observations of young children find that while a 2½-year-old can grasp a crayon and scribble with it, by the age of 4 years, s/he can draw a picture we recognize as human. The typical 4-year-old drawing of a human being is called the "tadpole person" because it has no body, a large head, and stick limbs. Between the ages of 3 and 4 years, children typically make a transition from scribbling to producing tadpole person drawings. This development is enabled by greater development in motor control and eye-hand coordination, among other variables. Between the ages of 4 and 5 years, children make another transition by progressing from drawing tadpole persons to drawing complete figures with heads and bodies. Howard Gardner, psychologist and author of the Multiple Intelligences theory, stated that children achieve a "summit of artistry" by the end of their preschool years. He describes their drawings as "characteristically colorful, balanced, rhythmic, and expressive, conveying something of the range and...vitality associated with artistic mastery." (1980)

Periods of communication development

Individual differences dictate a broad range of language development that is still normal. However, parents observing noticeably delayed language development in their children should consult professionals. Typically, babies respond to hearing their names by 6 months of age; turn their heads and eyes toward the sources of human voices they hear; and respond accordingly to friendly and angry tones of voice. By the age of 12 months, toddlers can usually understand and follow simple directions, especially when these are

- 12 -

accompanied by physical and/or vocal cues. They can intentionally use one or more words with the correct meaning. By the age of 18 months, a normally developing child usually has acquired a vocabulary of roughly 5 to 20 words. 18-month-old children use nouns in their speech most of the time. They are very likely to repeat certain words and/or phrases over and over. At this age, children typically are able to follow simple verbal commands without needing as many visual or auditory cues as at 12 months.

By the time most children reach the age of 2 years, they have acquired a vocabulary of about 150 to 300 words. They can name various familiar objects found in their environments. They are able to use at least two prepositions in their speech, for example in, on, and/or under. 2-year-olds typically combine the words they know into short sentences. These sentences tend to be mostly noun-verb or verb-noun combinations (e.g. "Daddy work," "Watch this"). They may also include verb-preposition combinations (e.g. "Go out," "Come in"). By the age of 2 years, children use pronouns, such as I, me, and you. They typically can use at least two such pronouns correctly. A normally developing 2-year-old will respond to some commands, directions, or questions, such as "Show me your eyes" or "Where are your ears?"

By the time they are 3 years old, most normally developing children have acquired vocabularies of between 900 and 1,000 words. Typically they correctly use the pronouns I, me, and you. They use more verbs more frequently. They apply past tenses to some verbs and plurals to some nouns. 3-year-olds usually can use at least three prepositions; the most common are in, on, and under. The normally developing 3-year-old knows the major body parts and can name them. 3-year-olds typically use 3-word sentences with ease. Normally, adults should find approximately 90 percent of what a 3-year-old says to be intelligible. Children this age comprehend most simple questions about their activities and environments and can answer questions about what they should do when they are thirsty, hungry, sleepy, hot, or cold. They can tell about their experiences in ways that adults can generally follow. By the age of 3 years, children should also be able to tell others their name, age, and sex.

When normally developing children are 4 years old, most know the names of animals familiar to them. They can use at least four prepositions in their speech (e.g. in, on, under, to, from, etc.). They can name familiar objects in pictures, and they know and can identify one color or more. Usually they are able to repeat four-syllable words they hear. They verbalize as they engage in their activities, which Vygotsky dubbed "private speech." Private speech helps young children think through what they are doing, solve problems, make decisions, and reinforce the correct sequences in multistep activities. When presented with contrasting items, 4-year-olds can understand comparative concepts like bigger and smaller. At this age, they are able to comply with simple commands without the target stimuli being in their sight (e.g. "Put those clothes in the hamper" [upstairs]). 4-year-old children will also frequently repeat speech sounds, syllables, words, and phrases, similar to 18-month-olds' repetitions but at higher linguistic and developmental levels.

Once most children have reached the age of 5 years, their speech has expanded from the emphasis of younger children on nouns, verbs, and a few prepositions, and is now characterized by many more descriptive words, including adjectives and adverbs. 5-year-olds understand common antonyms, e.g. big/little, heavy/light, long/short, hot/cold. They can now repeat longer sentences they hear, up to about nine words. When given three consecutive, uninterrupted commands, the typical 5-year-old can follow these without forgetting one or two. At age 5 most children have learned simple concepts of time like today, yesterday, tomorrow; day, morning, afternoon, night; and before, after, and later. 5-year-olds typically speak in relatively long sentences, and normally should be incorporating some compound sentences (with more than one independent clause) and complex sentences (with one or more independent and dependent clauses). 5-year-old children's speech is also grammatically correct most of the time.

Language and communication development depend strongly on the language a child develops within the first five years of life. During this time, three developmental periods are observed. At birth, the first period begins. This period is characterized by infant crying and gazing. Babies communicate their sensations and emotions through these behaviors, so they are expressive; however, they are not yet intentional. They indirectly indicate their needs through expressing how they feel, and when these needs are met, these communicative behaviors are reinforced. These expressions and reinforcement are the foundations for the later development of intentional communication. This becomes possible in the second developmental period, between 6 and 18 months. At this time, infants become able to coordinate their attention visually with other people relative to things and events, enabling purposeful communication with adults. During the third developmental period, from 18 months on, children come to use language as their main way of communicating and learning. Preschoolers can carry on conversations, exercise self-control through language use, and conduct verbal negotiations.

Human language abilities

Language and communication abilities are integral parts of human life that are central to learning, successful school performance, successful social interactions, and successful living. Human language ability begins before birth: the developing fetus can hear not only internal maternal sounds, but also the mother's voice, others' voices, and other sounds outside the womb. Humans have a natural sensitivity to human sounds and languages from before they are born until they are about 4½ years old. These years are critical for developing language and communication. Babies and young children are predisposed to greater sensitivity to human sounds than other sounds, orienting them toward the language spoken around them. Children absorb their environmental language completely, including vocal tones, syntax, usage, and emphasis. This linguistic absorption occurs very rapidly. Children's first 2½ years particularly involve amazing abilities to learn language including grammatical expression.

Oral language skills achievements

Crucial oral language development skills enable children to (1) communicate by listening and responding to others' speech; (2) comprehend meanings of numerous words and concepts encountered in their listening and reading; (3) acquire information on subjects they are interested in learning about; and (4) use specific language to express their own thoughts and ideas. Research finds young children's ability to listen to, understand, and use spoken and written language is associated with their later reading, spelling, and writing literacy achievement. Infants typically begin developing oral language skills, which continue developing through life. Babies develop awareness of and attend to adult speech, and soon begin communicating their needs via gestures and speech sounds. Toddlers express emotions and ideas and solicit information via language. They start uttering simple sentences, asking questions, and giving opinions regarding their likes and dislikes. Young

- 14 -

preschoolers expand their vocabularies from hearing others' speech and from books. They describe past and possible future events and unseen objects; tell fictional/"make-believe" stories; and use complete sentences and more complex language.

Adults' narration of child activities and actions

One oral language development technique adults can use is to narrate, i.e. describe what a child is doing as s/he does it. For example, a caregiver can say, "I see you're spreading paste on the back of your paper flower—not too much so it's lumpy, but not too little so it doesn't stick. Now you're pressing the flower onto your poster board. It sticks—good work!" Hence narration can be incorporated as prelude and segue to verbal positive reinforcement. This promotes oral language development by introducing and illustrating syntaxes. Communicating locations and directionality employs verbs and prepositions. Describing intensity and manner employs adverbs. Labeling objects/actions that are currently present/taking place with new vocabulary words serves immediately to place those words into natural contexts, facilitating more authentic comprehension of word meanings and better memory retention. Caregivers/teachers can narrate children's activities during formal instructional activities and informal situations like outdoor playtime, snack time, and cleanup time, and subsequently converse with them about what they did.

Personal narratives

Personal narratives are the way that young children relate their experiences to others by telling the stories of what happened. The narrative structure incorporates reporting components such as: who was involved; where the events took place; and what happened. Understanding and using this structure is crucial to young children for their communication; however, many young children cannot follow or apply this sequence without scaffolding (temporary support as needed) from adults. Adults can ask young children guiding questions to facilitate and advance narratives. They can also provide learning tools that engage children's visual, tactile (touch), and kinesthetic (body position and movement) senses. This reinforces narrative use, increases the depth of scaffolding, and motivates children's participation. Children learn to play the main character; describe the setting; sequence plot actions; and use words and body language to express emotions. Topic-related action sequences or "social stories" are important for preschoolers to comprehend and express to promote daily transitions and self-regulation. Such conversational skills attainment achieves milestones in both linguistic and emotional-social development.

Play-based activities

When young children play, they often enact scenarios. Play scenarios tell stories that include who is involved, where they are, what happens, why it happens, and how the "actors" feel about it. Children engage in planning when they decide first what their playing will be about; which children are playing which roles; and who is doing what. This planning and the thought processes involved reflect narrative thinking and structure. Children who experience difficulties with planning play are more likely to avoid participating or to participate only marginally. Since playing actually requires these thought and planning processes, children who do not play spontaneously can be supported in playing by enabling them to talk about potential narratives/stories as foundations for play scenarios. When conflicts emerge during play, conversation is necessary to effect needed change. Narrative development constitutes gradual plot development; play conflicts are akin to fictional/personal narrative problems and result in changed feelings. Adults can help young children discuss problems, identify the changed feeling they cause, and discuss plans/actions for resolution.

Conversation with young children

Natural vs. intentional conversation
Children enjoy conversing with significant adults, including parents, caregivers, and teachers; and they require practice with doing so. Caregivers tend to talk with young children naturally, sometimes even automatically, throughout the day, which helps children develop significant language skills. However, caregivers can enhance young children's oral language development further through intentional conversations. One element of doing this is establishing an environment that gives the children many things to talk about and many reasons to talk. Another element of intentionally promoting oral language skills development is by engaging in shared conversations. When parents and caregivers share storybook reading with young children, this affords a particularly good springboard for shared conversations. Reading and conversing together are linguistic interactions supplying foundations for children's developing comprehension of numerous word meanings. Researchers find such abundant early word comprehension is a critical basis for later reading comprehension. Asking questions, explaining, requesting what they need, communicating feelings, and learning to listen to others talk are some important ways whereby children build listening, understanding, and speaking skills.

Elements that adults should include in their conversations with young children
Adults should converse with young children so the children get practice with: hearing and using rich and abstract vocabulary and increasingly complex sentences; using language to express ideas and ask questions for understanding; and using language to answer questions about past, future, and absent things rather than only about "here-and-now" things. To ensure they incorporate these elements in their conversations, adults can consider the following: in the home, care setting, or classroom, whose voices are heard most often and who does the most talking; the child, not the adult, should be talking at least half of the time. Adults should be using rich language with complex structures when conversing with young children. Adults should be talking with, not at children; the conversation should be shared equally rather than adults doing all the talking while children listen to them. Adults should also ask young children questions, rather than just telling them things. Additionally, adult questions should require that children use language to formulate and communicate abstract ideas.

Benefits of adults having 1:1 conversations
When parents, caregivers, or teachers converse 1:1 with individual children, children reap benefits not as available in group conversations. Caregivers should therefore try to have such individual conversations with each child daily. In daycare and preschool settings, some good times for caregivers to do this include when children arrive and leave; during shared reading activities with one or two children; and during center time. 1:1 talk allows the adult to repeat what the child says for reinforcement. It allows the adult to extend what the child said by adding more information to it, like new vocabulary words, synonyms, meanings, or omitted details. It allows the adult to revise what the child said by restating or recasting it. It allows the child to hear his or her own ideas and thoughts reflected back to them when the adult restates them. Moreover, 1:1 conversation allows adults to contextualize the

- 16 -

discussion accordingly with an individual child's understanding. It also allows adults to elicit children's comprehension of abstract concepts.

Extended conversations and turn-taking

When adults engage young children in extended conversations including taking many "back-and-forth" turns, these create the richest dialogues for building oral language skills. Adults make connections with and build upon children's declarations and questions. Adults model richer descriptive language by modifying/adding to children's original words with new vocabulary, adjectives, adverbs, and varying sentences with questions and statements. For example, a child shows an adult his/her new drawing, saying: "This is me and Gran in the garden," the adult can build on this/invite the child to continue: "What is your gran holding?" The child identifies what they planted: "Carrot seeds. Gran said to put them in the dirt so they don't touch." The adult can then encourage the child's use of language to express abstract thoughts: "What could happen if the seeds were touching?" The adult can then extend the conversation through discussion with the child about how plants grow or tending gardens. This introduces new concepts, builds children's linguistic knowledge, and helps them learn to verbalize their ideas.

Attaining in-depth comprehension of word meanings

To support deeper word-meaning comprehension, teachers can give multiple definitions and examples for the same word and connect new vocabulary with children's existing knowledge. For example, a teacher conducting a preschool classroom science experiment incorporates new scientific concepts with new vocabulary words and conversational practice: pouring water on a paper towel, the teacher asks children what is happening to the water. A child answers, "It's going into the paper." The teacher asks how. Another child says, "The paper's soaking it up." The teacher confirms this, teaches the word "absorb," compares the paper to a sponge, and asks how much more water will be absorbed. A child responds probably no more since water is already dripping out. The teacher pours water on a plastic lid, asking if it absorbs. Children respond, "No, it slides off." Confirming, the teacher teaches the word "repel." This teacher has introduced new science concepts and new vocabulary words; engaged the children in conversation; related new concepts and words to existing knowledge; and added information to deepen comprehension.

Topics that young children enjoy

Personal content is important with young children, who enjoy talking about themselves; e.g., what their favorite color is or where they got their new shirt; about their activities, like what they are constructing with Legos or shaping with Play-Doh; or about familiar events and things that access their knowledge, like their family activities and experiences with neighbors and friends. Here is an example of how a teacher can make use of children's conversation to reinforce it, expand it, and teach new vocabulary and grammar. The teacher asks a child what s/he is building and the child answers, "A place for sick animals." The teacher asks, "You mean an animal hospital [or vet clinic]?" and the child confirms. When a child says someone was taken to a hospital "in the siren," the teacher corrects the usage: "They took him to the hospital in the ambulance with the siren was sounding?" This recasts "siren" with the correct word choice, "ambulance." It incorporates "siren" correctly and extends the statement to a complete sentence.

Storytelling

<u>Organize thoughts, practice new vocabulary, and exercise imagination</u>
Young children like to communicate about their personal life experiences. When they can do this through narrative structure, it helps them use new words they are learning, organize their thoughts to express them coherently, and engage their imaginative powers. Teachers/caregivers can supply new words they need; model correct syntax for sentences by elaborating on or extending child utterances and asking them questions; and build further upon children's ideas. For example, a teacher asks a child what they did at her sister's birthday party. When the child describes the cake and makes gestures for a word she doesn't know, the teacher supplies "candles," which the child confirms and repeats. When the child then offers, "Mom says be careful with candles," the teacher asks what could happen if you're not careful, the child replies that candles can start a fire. In this way, teachers give young children models of sentence structure, teach vocabulary, and guide children in expressing their thoughts in organized sequences that listeners can follow.

Shared reading of books

When teachers share books with preschoolers, they can ask questions and discuss the content, giving great opportunities for building oral language through conversation. Books with simple text and numerous, engaging illustrations best invite preschoolers to talk about the characters and events in the pictures, and the plotlines they hear. Children's listening and speaking skills develop; they learn new information and concepts; their vocabularies increase; and their ability to define words and explain their meanings is enhanced through shared reading. Many children's books include rich varieties of words that may not occur in daily conversation, used in complete-sentence contexts. Teachers should provide preschoolers with fictional and nonfictional books; poetry and storybooks; children's reference books like picture dictionaries/encyclopedias; and "information books" covering single topics like weather, birds, reptiles, butterflies, or transportation whereby children can get answers to questions or learn topical information. Detailed illustrations, engaging content, and rich vocabulary are strong elements motivating children to develop oral language and understand how to form sentences, how to use punctuation, and how language works.

Abstract thought is stimulated by asking young children to think about things not observed and/or current. During/after sharing books, teachers can ask children what else might happen in the story; what they imagine the story's characters could be feeling or thinking—which also engages their imaginations; and ask them the meaning of the story's events using questions necessitating children's use of language to analyze this meaning. Teachers can ask younger children vocabulary words: "What did we call this animal?" and encourage them to use language by asking them to describe story details, like "How do the firemen reach people up high in the building?" Once younger children are familiar with a story, teachers can activate and monitor their retention and recall: "Do you remember what happened to Arthur the day before that?" Teachers can ask older children to predict what they think will happen next in a story; to imagine extensions beyond the story ("What would you do if...?"); and make conclusions regarding why characters feel/behave as they do.

According to researchers' findings, the effectiveness of shared reading experiences is related to the ways that adults read with young children. Rather than merely labeling objects or events with vocabulary words, teachers should ask young children to recall the shared reading, which monitors their listening comprehension and retention abilities. They should ask children to predict what will happen next based on what already happened in a book; speculate about what could possibly happen; describe characters, actions, events, and information from the shared reading; and ask their own questions about it. Shared reading with small groups of 1–3 children permits teachers to involve each child in the book by questioning and conversing with them about the pictures and plots. To teach vocabulary, teachers can tell children word meanings; point to illustrations featuring new words; relate new words to words the children already know; give multiple, varied examples of new words; and encourage children to use new words they learn in their conversations.

Young children develop preferences for favorite books. Once they know a story's plot, they enjoy discussing their knowledge. Teachers can use this for extended conversations. They can ask children who the characters are; where the story takes place; and why characters do things and events occur. They can ask specific questions requiring children to answer how much/how many/how far a distance/how long a time, etc. Teachers can also help children via prompting to relate stories to their own real-life experiences. In a thematic approach, teachers can select several books on the same theme, like rain forests or undersea life. This affords richer extended conversations about the theme. It also allows teachers to "recycle" vocabulary by modeling and encouraging use of thematically related words, which enhances memory and in-depth comprehension of meanings. Teachers can plan activities based on book themes, like painting pictures/murals, sculpting, making collages, or constructing models, which gives children additional motivation to use the new language they learn from shared readings of books.

New experiences and information

Topics with interesting, rich content that stimulate young children's thinking are likelier to encourage them to engage in extended conversations. A teacher can base such conversations on experiences like exposure to interesting new objects/field trips. It is also a critical skill for young children to have conversations about past, future, and distant events. Their thinking is mostly concrete; getting them to discuss things that are not right here, right now, promotes their ability to think abstractly. For example, a teacher asks children what they saw visiting a construction site. One child says "a giant thing;" another supplies the word "crane;" a third specifies, "But a truck, not a bird." The teacher asks what it was doing, and one child says, "Picking up a big thing." The teacher supplies the term "I-beam," and asks, "Why do you think that's its name?" A child volunteers, "Because it looks like a big 'I'?" The teacher affirms the response and then asks the children what they think I-beams are used for in construction.

Print awareness

Even before they have learned how to read, young children develop print awareness, which constitutes children's first preparation for literacy. Children with print awareness realize that spoken language is represented by the markings on paper (or computer screens). They understand that the information in printed books adults read comes from the words, not the pictures. Children who have print awareness furthermore realize that print serves different functions within different contexts. They know that restaurant menus give information about the foods available; books tell stories or provide information; some signs show the names of stores, hotels, or restaurants, and other signs give traffic directions or danger warnings. Moreover, print awareness includes knowledge of how print is organized, e.g. that words are combinations of letters and have spaces in between them. Children with print awareness also know that [English] print is read from left to right and top to bottom; book pages are numbered; words convey ideas and meaning; and reading's purpose is to understand those ideas and acquire that meaning.

One way in which a teacher can get an idea of whether or to what extent a young child has developed print awareness is to provide the child with a storybook. Then the teacher can ask the child the following: "Show me the front of the book. Show me the back of the book. Show me the spine of the book. Where is the book's title? Where in the book are you supposed to start reading it? Show me a letter in the book. Now show me a word. Show me the first word of a sentence. Can you show me the last word of a sentence? Now will you show me the first word on a page? Please show me the last word on a page. Can you show me a punctuation mark? Can you show me a capital letter? Can you find a small letter/lowercase letter?" The teacher should also praise each correct response, supply the correct answers for incorrect responses, and review corrected answers.

Teachers should show young children the organization of books and the purpose of reading. When they read to them, they should use books with large print, which are more accessible for young children to view and begin to learn reading. Storybook text should use words familiar/predictable to young children. While reading together, teachers should point out high-frequency words like the, a, is, was, you; and specific letters, words, and punctuation marks in a story. Teachers can use index cards to label objects, areas, and centers in the classroom, pairing pictorial labels with word labels, and direct children's attention to them. They can invite preschoolers to play with printed words by making greeting cards, signs, or "writing" shopping lists and personal letters. They should point out print in calendars, posters, and signs. Also, teachers can have children narrate a story using a wordless picture book; write down their narrative on a poster; and reinforce the activity with a reward related to the story (e.g. eating pancakes after narrating the book Pancakes).

Environmental print

Street signs, traffic signs, store and restaurant names, candy wrappers, food labels, product logos, etc.—all the print we see in everyday life—are environmental print. Just as parents often play alphabetic games with children in the car ("Find something starting with A...with B..." etc.), adults can use environmental print to enhance print awareness and develop reading skills. They can ask children to find letters from their names on colorful cereal boxes. They can select one sign type, e.g. stop, one-way, or pedestrian crossing, and ask children to count how many they see during a car trip. They can have children practice reading each sign and talk about the phonemes (speech sounds) each letter represents. Adults can take photos of different signs and compile them into a little book for children to "read." By cutting familiar words from food labels, they can teach capitalized and lowercase letters; associate letters with phonemes; have children read the words; and sort words by their initial letters and by categories (signs, foods, etc.).

Reading a story aloud

Before reading a story aloud, adults should tell young children its title and the author's name. Then they can ask the children what an author does (children should respond "write stories" or something similar). Giving the illustrator's name, the adult also can then ask the children what illustrators do (children should respond "draw pictures" or something similar). Holding up the book, an adult can identify the front, spine, and back and ask the children if we start reading at the front or back (children should respond "at the front"). Adults can show young children the illustration on the front cover of the book and ask them, "From this picture, what do you think is going to happen in this story?" and remind them to answer this question in complete sentences. These exchanges before reading a story aloud activate children's fundamental knowledge regarding print and books, as well as the last example's exercising their imagination and language use.

When a teacher is reading a story aloud to young children, after reading each page aloud, s/he should have the children briefly discuss the picture illustrations on each page and how they relate to what the teacher just read aloud. After they read aloud each plot point, action, event, or page, they should ask the children open-ended (non yes/no) questions about what they just heard. This monitors and supports listening comprehension and memory retention/recall and stimulates expressive language use. When children associate something in the story with their own life experiences, teachers should have them explain the connection. As they read, teachers should stop periodically and ask the children to predict or guess what will happen next before continuing. This promotes abstract thinking, understanding of logical sequences, and also exercises the imagination. After reading the story, teachers should ask children whether they liked it and why/why not, prompting them to answer using complete sentences. This helps children to organize their thoughts and opinions and to develop clear, grammatical, complete verbal expression.

Just before reading a story aloud to young students, the teacher should identify vocabulary words in the story that s/he will need to go over with the children. The teacher can write these words on the board or on strips of paper. Discussing these words before the reading will give the children definitions for new/unfamiliar words, and help them understand word meanings within the story's context. Teachers can also give young children some open-ended questions to consider when listening to the story. They will then repeat these questions during and after the reading. Questions should NOT be ones children can answer with yes/no. When discussing vocabulary words, the teacher can also ask the children to relate words to personal life experiences. For example, with the word fish, some children may want to talk about going fishing with parents. Teachers can encourage children to tell brief personal stories, which will help them relate the story they are about to hear to their own real-life experience, making the story more meaningful.

Alphabetic principle

The alphabetic principle is the concept that letters and letter combinations represent speech sounds. Children's eventual reading fluency requires knowing these predictable relationships of letters to sounds, which they can then apply to both familiar and unfamiliar words. Young children's knowing the shapes and names of letters predicts their later reading success: knowing letter names is highly correlated with the ability to view words as letter sequences and to remember written/printed words' forms. Children must first be able to recognize and name letters to understand and apply the alphabetic principle. Young children learn letter names first, via singing the alphabet song and reciting rhymes and alphabetical jump-rope chants ("A my name is Alice, I come from Alabama, and I sell Apples; B my name is Betty..." etc.). They learn letter shapes after names, through playing with lettered blocks, plastic/wood/cardboard letters, and alphabet books. Once they can recognize and name letters, children learn letter sounds after names and shapes and spellings after sounds.

To help young children understand that written or printed letters represent corresponding speech sounds, teachers should teach relationships between letters and sounds separately, in isolation, and should teach these directly and explicitly. They should give young children daily opportunities during lessons to practice with letter-sound relationships. These opportunities for practice should include cumulative reviews of sound-letter relationships they have already learned and new letter-sound relationships as well. Adults should begin early in providing frequent opportunities to young children for applying their increasing knowledge and understanding of sound-letter relationships to early experiences with reading. They can do this by providing English words that are spelled phonetically (i.e. spelled the same way that they sound) and have meanings that are already familiar to the young learners.

Self-concept

Self-concept development begins during early childhood. Children come to identify characteristics, abilities, values, and attitudes that they feel define them. From 18–36 months, children develop the Categorical Self. This is a concrete view of oneself, usually related to observably opposite characteristics, e.g. child versus adult, girl versus boy, short versus tall, and good versus bad. A four-year-old might say, "I'm shorter than Daddy. I have blue eyes. I can help Mommy clean house!" Young children can also describe emotional and attitudinal aspects of self-concept, e.g. "I like playing with Joshua. I'm happy today." Preschoolers do not usually integrate these aspects into a unified self-portrait, however. Also, many preschoolers do not yet realize one person can incorporate opposite qualities; a person is either good or bad to them, rather than having both good and bad qualities. The Remembered Self develops with long-term memory, including autobiographical memories and things adults have told them, to comprise one's life story. The Inner Self is the child's private feelings, desires, and thoughts.

Self-concept and self-esteem

Young children's self-concepts are founded on observable, readily defined, mainly concrete factors. Many young children also experience much adult encouragement. Because their self-concepts are more simple and concrete than those of older children and adults and because they typically receive abundant encouragement and positive reinforcement, preschoolers often have fairly high self-esteem, i.e. judgment regarding their own value. In general, young children tend to have positive, optimistic attitudes that they can learn something new, finish tasks, and succeed if they persist in their attempts. Self-esteem related specifically to one's ability to perform a given task is sometimes called "achievement-related attribution." Albert Bandura called it "self-efficacy." Young children derive self-esteem from multiple sources, including their relationships with their parents; their friendships; their abilities and achievements in tasks involving playing and helping others; their physical/athletic abilities; and their achievements in preschool/school.

Phonics instruction

Because children display individual differences in their speeds of learning sound-to-letter relationships, instruction should consider this; there is no set rate. Generally, a reasonable pace ranges from two to four sound-letter relationship per week. Relationships vary in utility: many words contain the sounds/letters m, a, t, s, p, and h, which are high-utility; but x as in box, gh as in through, ey as in they, and the sound of a as in want are lower-utility. High-utility sound-letter relationships should be taught first. Teachers should first introduce consonant relationships using f, m, n, r, and s, which are continuous sounds children can produce in isolation with less distortion than word-initial or word-medial stops like p, b, t, d, k, and g. Teachers should also introduce similar-sounding letters like b and v or i and e, and similar-looking letters like b and d or p and g, separately to prevent confusion. Single consonants versus clusters/blends should be introduced in separate lessons. Blends should incorporate sound-letter relationships children already know.

Temperament types

Psychologists studied the behavior of infants and classified their characteristics into three types of temperaments: easy, difficult, and slow to warm up. The majority of infants are easy babies. When they cry from hunger/needing changing/being tired/feeling discomfort/needing cuddling/attention, they are easily soothed by having these needs met. They typically sleep well. While they experience normal negative emotions, their predominant mood is good. Other than normal stranger anxiety at applicable ages, they respond positively to meeting people. In contrast, difficult babies are more likely to cry longer and be much harder to soothe. It is often hard to get them to sleep, and they may sleep fitfully, with many interruptions and/or for shorter times. They are more easily frightened by strange/new people and things, and more easily upset overall. Slow to warm up babies can initially seem difficult by not being as immediately responsive to people other than their parents like easy babies. However, given some time to adjust, they eventually "warm up" to new people and situations.

Learning style

Young children with normal development learn in the same chronological sequences and learn the same types of skills. Even those with delayed development, as with intellectual disabilities, learn the same things in the same order, but simply at a slower rate and hence at later ages; and those with severe/profound impairment may never achieve certain developmental milestones. However, one aspect of learning that varies is learning style. For example, some children approach learning in a primarily visual manner. They focus on what they see and how things look. They learn best given visual stimuli, like colorful objects, pictures, and graphics. They understand abstract concepts and relationships better when these are illustrated visually. Other children approach learning in a primarily haptic or tactile way. They focus on textures and movements, learning through touch and kinesthetic senses. They learn best given concrete things to explore and manipulate, and physical activities to perform. They learn abstract concepts and relationships better through handling materials and engaging in physical movements and actions.

External and internal variables

External variables
The way young children see themselves is affected by the feedback they receive from other people. When adults like parents, caregivers, and teachers give young children positive responses to their efforts—whether they succeed initially or not—the children are more likely to develop positive self-concepts, engendering higher self-esteem, and greater self-efficacy, the belief that they have the competency to succeed at a specific task or activity. On the other hand, when adults frequently give punitive/judgmental/indifferent/otherwise negative responses to young children's efforts, children develop poorer self-images. They feel they are not valued/good/important/worthy. They develop lower self-esteem, and

their self-efficacy is weaker; they come to expect failure when they attempt tasks and may not even try. Peers also affect young children's self-concepts and self-esteem. When friends and classmates include a child in activities, this promotes a positive self-image and higher self-esteem and self-efficacy. If peers exclude, tease, or bully a young child, this can cause low self-esteem, make their self-concepts more negative, and lower their self-efficacy.

Internal variable

One major internal influence on self-concept is a child's basic temperament. Easy, difficult, and slow-to-warm-up temperaments in babies continue into early childhood (and throughout life). For example, children having easy temperaments are better prepared for coping with challenges and frustration. When they encounter difficulty attempting new tasks, they do not give up as easily and are more persistent. They are thus more likely to develop self-concepts of being good, valuable, and successful and hence have higher self-esteem. Since they experience more success through persistence, they develop greater self-efficacy, i.e. belief in their competence to perform specific tasks. Children with more difficult temperaments become frustrated more easily, after fewer attempts, and give up trying in discouragement or require extra help to perform new or challenging tasks. They are more at risk for believing they cannot succeed and hence are not valuable, leading to their developing lower self-esteem. This also affects self-efficacy: they are more likely to doubt their ability to perform a specific proposed task.

Locus of control

Psychologist Julian Rotter originated the term and concept of locus of control. It refers to the place (locus) where we attribute causes for outcomes we experience, either externally or internally. An external locus control is something outside of us—another person and/or his/her actions; an environmental event; or an unknown but exterior influence, like good/bad luck or random chance. An internal locus of control is something inside of us—our native ability, our motivation, or our effort. For example, blaming another for failing—"The teacher gave me something too hard/wouldn't help me/didn't tell me how to do it" or "Johnny was bothering me" are examples of external locus of control. Blaming conditions, e.g. "It was too dark/hot/cold/noisy/the sun was in my eyes" is also external. Individuals may also attribute successes externally: "The teacher helped me" or "Johnny showed me how" or "I was lucky." Blaming/crediting oneself for failure/success is internal locus of control: "I didn't study the new words" or "I'm stupid" with failures or "I worked hard"/"I'm smart" with successes.

Freud's psychoanalytic theory of personality development

Freud's orientation toward personality development was psychosexual. He believed the most important factors were the focus of erotic energy, which shifted in each developmental stage, and the child's early relationship with parents. Freud formulated five stages of development: Oral, Anal, Phallic, Latency, and Genital. He found if infants and children successfully complete each stage, they are well-adjusted; if not, they become fixated on one stage. Freud said infants from birth to 18 months are in the first Oral stage: their focus of pleasure is on the mouth as they suck to nurse. If a baby's oral need to nurse is met appropriately, s/he will progress to the following stage. However, if an infant's feeding needs are met either inadequately or excessively, s/he can develop an oral fixation. Signs of this in later life include tendencies to overeat, drink too much, smoke, bite one's nails, talk excessively, and other orally focused activities. Oral personalities either become overly dependent and gullible; or, when resisting oral compulsions, become pessimistic and aggressive to others.

Freud's theory divided personality development into five stages, each based on the corresponding erogenous zone: Oral, Anal, Phallic, Latency, and Genital. Infants 0–18 months are in the Oral stage as the focus is on nursing. Children 18–36 months are in the second Anal stage. The focus of pleasure sensations is on the anus as they are engaged in toilet training. Society and parents demand they control retaining/expelling waste; they must learn to control anal stimulation. This can be a power struggle between child and parents. Children this age are also learning to assert their individual independence and will, mirroring the battle of wills over toileting. Success contributes to healthy development; when unsuccessful, individuals develop anal fixation. Signs of this in later life take two extremes: those who resisted parental control and asserted personal control by retaining their feces develop anal-retentive personalities, becoming rigid, controlling, and overly preoccupied with neatness and cleanliness. Conversely, those who asserted themselves by expelling their feces develop anal-expulsive personalities, with sloppy, messy, disorganized, defiant behavior.

Freud described developmental stages as focusing on particular erogenous zones. Nursing infants are in his Oral stage; toilet-training toddlers are in his Anal stage. His third stage, when children are aged 3–6 years, is the Phallic stage. Pleasure is focused on the genitals as children discover these. Freud focused his theory on males, proposing that at this age, boys develop unconscious sexual desires for their mothers and corresponding unconscious rivalries with their fathers for mother's attention. The rivalry represents aggression toward the father. Therefore they also unconsciously fear retaliation by the father in the form of castration. Freud named this the Oedipal conflict after the Greek tragic hero Oedipus, who unwittingly slew his father and married his mother. Since these unconscious impulses are socially unacceptable, boys resolve the conflict through a process Freud called "identification with the aggressor." This explains the common behavior of boys around ages 4–5, imitating and wanting to be "just like Daddy." They repress desires for mother and adopt masculine characteristics.

In his theory of personality development, Freud placed children ages 3–6 in his third Phallic stage when pleasure is focused on the genitals. He proposed that boys undergo an Oedipal conflict at this age, which he named after Greek tragedian Sophocles' Oedipus Rex, wherein the title character killed his father and married his mother. He said a boy unconsciously desires his mother, competing for her affection with his father, which equals aggression toward the father, and fears retaliation by the father through castration. He resolves these unacceptable impulses by "identifying with the aggressor," wanting to be like his father. Unsuccessful conflict resolution/fixation leads to later confusion/weakness of sexual identity, and either excessive or insufficient sexual activity. Because Freud focused only on males, later psychologists proposed a female counterpart, the Electra conflict. They pointed out how girls at the same ages become "Daddy's girls," often rejecting their mothers, and then around ages 4–5 want to be "just like Mommy," adopting feminine behaviors, paralleling male development. Freud rejected this notion.

Each of the stages in Freud's theory centered on an erogenous zone. Infants are in the Oral stage as they nurse; toddlers in the Anal stage as they are toilet-trained; preschoolers are in the Phallic stage as they focus on genital discovery, unconscious sexual impulses toward their opposite-sex parent, and unconscious aggressive impulses toward their same-sex parent, and resolving conflicts over these urges. Freud labeled the stage when children are six years old to puberty the Latency stage. During this time, children begin school. They are occupied with making new friends, developing new social skills; participating in learning, developing new academic skills; and learning school rules, developing acceptable societal behaviors. Freud said that children in the Latency stage repress their sexual impulses, deferring them while developing their cognitive and social skills takes priority. Thus sexuality is latent. From puberty on, children are in Freud's Genital stage, when sexuality reemerges with physical maturation and adolescents are occupied with developing intimate relationships with others.

Freud proposed that the personality is governed by three structures or forces: the Id, the Ego, and the Superego. The Id, the "pleasure principle," represents the source of our powerful, instinctual urges, such as sexual and aggressive impulses. It is necessary as it energizes us to act, but cannot go unrestrained. The Ego, the "reality principle," represents our sense of self within reality. It is necessary for telling us what will happen if we act on the Id's impulses and knowing how to control them to protect ourselves. The Superego, the "conscience," represents our sense of morality. It is necessary when Ego protects ourselves but not others, so we also control our social interactions to be ethical and nonharmful to others. For example, when a young child sees a cookie or a toy belonging to someone else, his Id says, "I want that." His Ego says, "If I take that and get caught, I will be in trouble." His Superego says, "Whether I get caught or not, stealing is wrong."

Developing sex/gender identity

Children's development of sexual/gender identification
While different psychological theories/schools of thought agree that sex as a social identity develops through the process of identification, they have different views and explanations for how children develop their social identities as boys or girls. In Freud's view, gender identity develops through processes of differentiation and affiliation. He said once children observe that certain other people have characteristics in common with themselves, they "endeavor to mold the ego after one that had been taken as a model." In other words, they identify with similar other people and try to attain the same attributes. Freud proposed that boys resolve their Oedipal conflicts through identification with the aggressor, i.e. adopting their fathers' characteristics and suppressing sexual impulses toward their mothers. While he focused exclusively on males in this respect, Neo-Freudian psychologists later proposed a female counterpart, the Electra conflict, wherein girls resolve desires for fathers by identifying with mothers and adopting their characteristics. In either case, children differentiate from their opposite-sex parent and identify/affiliate with their same-sex parent.

Processes of developing sex/gender identity
Albert Bandura and other proponents of social learning theory maintain that children learn through a process of observing other people's behavior, observing certain behaviors of others that are rewarded, and then imitating those behaviors to obtain similar rewards. The concept of rewards reinforcing behaviors, i.e. increasing the probability of repeating them, comes from behaviorism or learning theory. Social learning theory is based on behaviorism, but includes additional emphasis on the ideas that learning occurs within a social context and that social interactions are primary influences on learning. According to social learning theory, children observe that males and females engage in different behaviors. They additionally observe that boys and girls receive different rewards for their behaviors. Based

on these observations, children then imitate the behaviors appropriate to their own sex that they have seen rewarded in others of their sex to obtain the same rewards. Both behaviorist and social learning theories view gender identity development as being environmentally shaped by consequences; social learning theory focuses on the social environment.

General conclusions of psychologists

Various theories of development, such as psychoanalytic, behaviorist, cognitive, and social learning, have differing views of why and how children develop sexual/gender identities. To address these differences, psychologists have endeavored to produce some general conclusions about young children's self-concepts of gender. They find that during preschool ages, children gradually develop concepts of what being a girl or a boy in their culture means. These concepts become clearly articulated and shape their behaviors. Between the ages of 2 and 6, children are in the process of putting together the pieces of these gender concepts. Developing sex-appropriate behaviors and developing categories of gender roles both appear to be influenced by a combination and interaction of biological and sociological variables. Psychologists additionally conclude that children perform some mental matching process enabling them to isolate features they share in common with others, and that young children's abilities to observe, imitate, and categorize influence their later concepts of sex-appropriate behaviors. By ages 5–6, most children clearly identify with one sex or the other.

Ego defense mechanisms

Freud identified and described many ego defense mechanisms in his theory. He said these are ways the ego finds to cope with impulses threatening it, and hence the person. Just a few of these that can be apparent in young children's behavior include the following. Regression—for example, if a child has received parental attention exclusively for four years, but then the parents introduce a new baby, not only is parental attention divided between two children, but the baby naturally needs and gets more attention by being a helpless infant. If the child feels displaced/threatened by the younger sibling, s/he may regress from normal four-year-old behaviors to more infantile ones in a bid for similar attention. Projection—if a child feels threatened by experiencing inner aggressive impulses, e.g. hating another person, s/he may project these feelings onto that person, accusing, "You hate me!" Denial—if a child cannot accept feelings triggered by losing a loved one through divorce or death, s/he may deny reality: "S/he will come back."

Erik Erikson's psychosocial theory of human development

In each of Erikson's developmental stages, a central conflict must be resolved; success/failure dictates outcomes. Babies first develop basic trust or mistrust in the world during the first stage. Toddlers are in Erikson's second stage of Autonomy vs. Shame and Self-Doubt. In this stage, children 18 months—3 years are learning muscular control (walking, toilet-training) and developing moral senses of right/wrong. As they gain skills, they want to do more things independently, and they begin to assert their individual wills. Parents are familiar with the associated tantrums, "No!" and other common "Terrible Twos" behaviors. Children receiving appropriate parenting during this stage develop a sense of autonomy through being allowed to attempt tasks realistic for them; to fail and try again; and eventually to master them. Positive outcomes are will/willpower and self-control; negative outcomes are impulsivity and compulsion. Children with parenting at either extreme—being ignored and given no guidance or support; or overly controlled/directed, having everything done for them and never allowed freedom—develop shame, doubting their abilities.

Each of Erikson's nine developmental stages involves a "nuclear crisis" the individual must resolve; success or failure results in positive or negative outcomes. Babies develop basic trust or mistrust; toddlers develop autonomy or shame and self-doubt. Erikson's third stage, Initiative vs. Guilt, involves preschoolers. At this age, young children are exploring the environment further commensurately with their increasing physical/motor, cognitive, emotional, and social skills. They exercise imagination in make-believe/pretend play and pursue adventure. Having gained some control over their bodies in the previous stage, they now attempt to exercise control over their environments. When they succeed in this stage, the positive outcomes are purpose and direction. Children who receive adult disapproval for exerting control over their surroundings—either because they try to use too much control or because parents are overly controlling—feel guilt. Negative outcomes include excessive inhibition against taking action or ruthless, inconsiderate behavior at the opposite extreme.

Erikson formulated nine stages encompassing the entire human lifespan. The fourth stage corresponds to the end of the early childhood years, when children begin formal schooling. Erikson named this stage, which lasts from around ages 5–6 to puberty, Industry vs. Inferiority. Children in this stage are primarily occupied with learning new academic and social competencies as they attend school, meet more peers and adults, make new friends, and learn to interact in a wider environment. Whereas the focus of Stage 2, Autonomy vs. Shame and Doubt, was self-control and parents were the main relationship; and the focus of Stage 3, Initiative vs. Guilt, was environmental exploration and family was the main relationship; in Stage 4, Industry vs. Inferiority, the focus is on achievements and accomplishments. Friends, neighbors, school, and teachers are the most important relationships. Children's successful resolutions bring positive outcomes of competence and method; negative outcomes are narrowness of abilities and inertia (lack of activity).

Differences between Freud's and Erikson's developmental theories

Erikson's theory was based on Freud's, but whereas Freud's focus was psychosexual, Erikson's was psychosocial. Both emphasized early parent-child relationships. Freud believed the personality was essentially formed in childhood and proposed five stages through puberty and none thereafter; Erikson depicted lifelong development through nine stages. Each stage centers on a "nuclear conflict" to resolve, with positive/negative outcomes of successful/unsuccessful resolutions. Erikson's first, infancy stage (birth—18 months) is Basic Trust vs. Mistrust. When an infant's basic needs—such as being fed, changed, bathed, held/cuddled, having discomfort relieved, and receiving attention, affection, and interaction are met sufficiently and consistently, the baby develops basic trust in the world, gaining a sense of security, confidence, and optimism. The positive outcomes are hope and drive; negative outcomes are withdrawal and sensory distortion. If infant needs are inadequately and/or inconsistently met, the baby develops basic mistrust, with a sense of insecurity, worthlessness, and pessimism.

Lawrence Kohlberg's cognitive-developmental theory

Kohlberg had developed a cognitive theory of moral development, based upon and expanding the concepts of morality Piaget included in his theory of cognitive development.

Kohlberg also proposed a cognitive-developmental approach to children's acquisition of sex/gender roles. Piaget and Kohlberg discussed classification or categorization as one of the cognitive abilities that children develop. Just as they learn to categorize various things, e.g. foods, animals, people, etc., they learn that people include female and male categories. They then learn to categorize themselves as either female/girls or male/boys. When children are around 2 years old, they each begin to develop their distinctive sense of self. Once they have differentiated self from the rest of the world, they also begin to be able to develop complex mental concepts. These abilities enable them to develop self-concepts of gender. According to the cognitive-developmental view, once children have developed concepts of their sex/gender, these are maintained despite social contexts and are difficult to change.

Aggression relative to early childhood

Preschoolers typically demonstrate some aggressive behavior, which tends to peak around age 4. Instrumental Aggression is one basic type: younger preschoolers frequently shout, hit, or kick others to get concrete objects they want. Middle preschoolers are more likely to exhibit Hostile Aggression, i.e. getting even for wrongs or injuries they feel others have done to them. Hostile Aggression occurs in two subtypes: Overt and Relational. Overt Aggression involves physically harming others or threatening to do so, while Relational Aggression involves emotional/social harm, e.g. rejecting/excluding another from a group of friends or spreading malicious rumors about another. Young boys are more likely to engage in Overt Aggression, while young girls are more likely to engage in Relational Aggression. These gender preferences in aggressive behaviors tend to remain the same at all ages if aggression exists. While most young children eventually phase out aggression as they learn other ways of resolving social conflicts, some persist in verbally and/or physically aggressive behavior, causing problems.

Minimizing aggressive behavior in young children

While it is normal for preschoolers to exhibit some physical and verbal aggression until they have learned more mature ways of expressing feelings, getting what they want, and settling disputes, there are things adults can do to influence them such that aggressive behavior does not develop into a predominant method of social interaction. Adults set examples for children, and children learn by observing and imitating those examples. Therefore, parents, caregivers, and teachers should not model verbally and/or physically aggressive behaviors such as calling others names, yelling at others, or punishing others' undesirable behaviors using physical force. Not only should adults avoid disciplining children physically, they should also avoid physically and/or verbally violent interactions with other adults. Social learning theorist Albert Bandura proved that children who viewed violent videos imitated what they observed and engaged in more aggressive behavior, so adults should also prevent young children's exposure to violent TV programming and video games.

Prejudice and discrimination

Prejudice literally means prejudging, i.e. judging someone/something negatively before/without knowing anything about who/what one is judging. Prejudice gives rise to discrimination in that prejudiced ideas motivate unfair, i.e. discriminatory, behaviors toward others. Psychologist Albert Bandura, who developed social learning theory, identified the process whereby children acquire attitudes and behaviors they observe in others, which he named vicarious learning. Children commonly pick up beliefs, attitudes, and behaviors from adults around them, without applying any critical thinking to these. They are often not even aware of the attitudes and beliefs they assume in this way. Thus, they will engage in prejudicial attitudes and discriminatory behaviors without thinking through what they are doing. Though such behavior is not justified, children simply assume it is because of adults' examples. Thus, adults must carefully inspect their own beliefs and attitudes, as well as what they do and say, because these are what children will imitate.

Because many prejudicial attitudes exist in our society on both individualized and institutionalized levels, it is all too easy for children to absorb and emulate them. When children who have been victims of prejudice learn they were attacked not as individuals, but members of a group, this does not eliminate negative effects, but can help them see it in a different perspective. Adults can place prejudice and discrimination in their historical contexts so children realize they are not lone victims but part of a larger group. Correcting false beliefs, as in Albert Ellis's Rational-Emotive Behavior Therapy and other forms of cognitive-behavioral therapy, can be applied by adults' pointing out the irrational, flawed thinking involved and supplying examples contradicting that thinking. For example, if children have been influenced to think certain groups are less intelligent or lazier than others, adults can show them examples of many members of those groups with outstanding achievements in society. They can do this through book/video biographies, personal anecdotes, and introductions to living people.

Sources of prejudicial thinking
Prejudicial thinking about certain groups of people is uninformed and/or misinformed thinking. It is typically based on fear of the unknown due to lack of knowledge and/or fear due to erroneous beliefs about people. Thus, the best way to dispel prejudice is to provide information where there was none and/or to correct wrong information. When unfamiliar groups become more familiar and when wrong assumptions are corrected, people's misconceptions are replaced by reality and they become less afraid. For example, children having no experience with people from other racial, ethnic, or socioeconomic groups are likely to fear these people (as are many adults). Adults can help young children by furnishing them with many opportunities—not just isolated ones—to interact with people from diverse cultural and socioeconomic milieus. For children to experience true learning, which will supersede negative, uninformed first impressions, they must have multiple such social opportunities. School, outside classes, sports, and camp are activities affording such opportunities.

Combating cultural stereotypes and discrimination
When children experience stereotyping of and discrimination against their cultural group, adults can counter these negative reflections on the group by correcting erroneous opinions they have heard. By giving children plenty of examples of positive accomplishments by members of their group, they convey cultural pride, affording children a sense of empowerment. Adults should consistently model positive, constructive, and no-violent methods of addressing prejudice for children. If prejudice proves ongoing, caregivers and teachers must assertively advocate on behalf of children and their cultures to shut down prejudicial sources. If they hear young children furthering cultural stereotypes they have absorbed, adults should immediately correct their statements and behaviors, explaining why certain words and actions harm others and are unacceptable. Extended discussions with young children are important for putting prejudice into perspective and context to help them understand it. Adults can also apply behavioral methods, such as associating

- 30 -

prejudicial behaviors with consequences (e.g. losing a privilege or gaining work) and providing related learning activities to prevent repeated instances.

Bullying

Children who are bullied by others are victims of prejudicial thinking and discriminatory actions. Common negative effects of bullying include rage, feelings of hopelessness, anxiety, and depression. Left untreated, children with these feelings can develop suicidal ideations and actions as they grow older if bullying persists. When young, children have the additional problem of not yet knowing how to manage their negative feelings caused by others' aggression or even how to express them. Adults can give them much-needed help by assisting them in articulating their emotions openly but nonviolently. Adults must realize that young children, especially those who have experienced others' violent treatment, may not recognize that anger can be expressed in any ways other than violent ones. Based on their experience, children may internalize assumptions that they can only act out their anger through self-destructive behaviors. When adults consistently model positive, proactive ways of discussing negative emotions, children observe that more constructive behaviors are possible and learn to adopt these as more effective coping strategies.

Psychoanalytic theory

In his development of psychoanalytic theory, Freud (a physician) identified stages of childhood development according to the particular bodily zones where pleasure is focused during each age period. This identification still regularly informs early childhood care and educational practices. For example, infants are in the Oral stage, when nursing provides pleasure as well as nutrition and satisfying hunger. Knowing this, caregivers recognize that babies begin exploring their environments through oral routes. They thus will not punish mouthing of objects; will anticipate and prevent mouthing of unsafe/unsanitary objects; provide suitable objects and activities for oral inspection and orally oriented rewards. Toddlers engaged in toilet-training are in Freud's Anal stage. As they learn to control their bladders and bowels, they also learn to control their impulses and behaviors. Adults knowing this recognize toddlers' willful, stubborn behaviors as normal parts of the process of establishing individual identities and asserting their wishes. Thus, they will not punish these behaviors harshly/inappropriately, but strike a balance between permitting exploration and providing limits, guidance, and support.

According to Freud's theory, preschoolers are in his Phallic stage of psychosexual development. This is the time when they discover their own genitals, so caregivers and educators knowing this will not be distressed at young children's attention to and manipulation of their genitals, and their curiosity and interest in others' genitals as these are not abnormal (unless excessive). Adults who are also aware of Freud's Oedipal conflict in boys and other Neo-Freudian psychologists' corresponding Electra conflict in girls should be neither surprised nor upset when little boys first focus more attention on mothers/female caregivers, and later abandon these attentions to focus on imitating fathers/male caregivers. Freud would say they are demonstrating the Oedipal desire for the mother, which includes fear of castration by the father, and then resolving this conflict through identification with the aggressor/father. Neo-Freudians would say little girls are undergoing a similar process in favoring their fathers and subsequently identifying with their mothers.

Freud theorized that children are in his fourth Latency stage of development at around the same ages when they begin to attend formal schooling. Since Freud's emphasis on development was psychosexual, he identified an erogenous zone where pleasure was focused in each stage of development. The mouth, anus, and genitals are erogenous zones central to Freud's other developmental stages. However, in the stage he termed Latency, there is no erogenous zone of focus. This is because Freud believed that children's sexuality is repressed or submerged during this period. The child's attention is occupied at this time with learning new social and academic skills in the new environment of the school setting. Adults familiar with Freud's basic psychoanalytic concepts realize that children's focus shifts from their relationships with parents to their relationships with friends, classmates, teachers, and other adults during the Latency stage. Children are not rejecting/abandoning parents, but responding to widening social environments. They are more able to learn academic concepts and structures and more complex social interactions and behaviors.

Piaget's stages of cognitive development

According to Piaget's theory, infants are in the Sensorimotor stage of cognitive development. This means they learn through sensory input they get from the environment, motor actions they perform, and environmental feedback they receive from those actions. They also eventually coordinate their actions and reactions. For example, babies hear and attend to sounds; visually locate sound sources; and learn that some objects make sounds, like rattles. They learn to reach for, grasp, and manipulate objects. They learn when they shake a rattle, it makes a sound, and then repeat this action purposefully to generate the sound. Adults knowing these characteristics will provide infants with many toys they can manipulate, including toys that make noises/music, spin/twirl, or roll/bounce/fly; experiences affording input through all sensory modalities; and positive reinforcement when babies discover new body parts, objects, sights, sounds, textures, smells, and tastes; and demonstrate new behaviors interacting with these. They will not punish repetitious behaviors, like repeatedly throwing items from cribs/high-chair trays, which are part of learning in this stage.

Piaget's second cognitive-developmental stage is Preoperational. Toddlers and preschoolers in this stage typically begin to recognize rudimentary symbolic representation, i.e. that some objects represent other things. This understanding of symbols allows them to begin using words to represent things, people, feelings, and thoughts. Adults can support early childhood language development by frequently conversing with young children, reading books to them, introducing and explaining new vocabulary words, and playing games involving naming and classifying things. Children in this stage also begin pretend/make-believe play through understanding symbols; adults can encourage and support this play, which develops imagination and planning abilities. Preoperational children's thinking is intuitive, not logical; adults understanding this will not expect them to follow/use logical sequences such as doing arithmetic, as they cannot yet perform mental operations. Adults familiar with Piaget's concept of egocentrism realize Preoperational children cannot see others' viewpoints. They thus engage children's attention/interest by beginning from topics related to children's personal selves and activities.

Magical thinking

According to Piaget, magical thinking is the belief that one's thoughts make external events happen. He identified this as a common characteristic of the way children in his

- 32 -

Preoperational stage think. Piaget said that preschool children have not yet developed the cognitive ability to perform mental operations. Because they cannot follow or apply logical thought processes, their thinking is irrational and intuitive rather than organized and based on real-world, empirical observations. For example, a Preoperational child may believe that something good happened because s/he wished hard enough for it. Preschoolers also commonly believe their saying/thinking/feeling/wishing something bad toward another caused the other's misfortune. They often blame themselves for divorce or death in the family, thinking these happened because they were "bad." Adults should explain to young children that what they wished, thought, felt, or said did not cause good or bad events, and reassign causes external to the child, e.g. "Mommy and Daddy were not getting along with each other"/"Grandpa was sick"/"It was an accident, not anybody's fault."

Egocentrism and animism as characteristic of Preoperational children

Preoperational children are egocentric, i.e. they view everything as revolving around themselves. Adults aware of this understand that most two-year-olds, for example, neither want to share with others nor understand why they should. Egocentrism also means being unable to see others' perspectives. Adults who take this ability for granted may not realize the simplicity of both some early childhood problems and their solutions. For example, when a preschooler does something physically or emotionally hurtful to another, adults can guide identification of consequences: "Look at her face now. How do you think she feels?" and then guide perspective-taking: "How would you feel if somebody hit you like you just hit Sally?" This has not occurred to the preschooler, but once s/he is guided to think of it, it can be a revelation. Animism is Preoperational children's attributing human qualities to inanimate objects. Many children's books and TV shows accordingly appeal to young children by animating letters, numbers, or objects (e.g. SpongeBob SquarePants).

Concrete Operations stage vs. Preoperational stage

Piaget said that while preschoolers are in the Preoperational stage and do not think logically because they cannot yet perform mental operations, this ability emerges in the Concrete Operations stage, which tends to coincide with elementary school ages. Concrete Operational children can follow and apply logical sequences to concrete objects they can see and manipulate. This is why they can begin learning mathematical concepts and procedures like addition and subtraction, and grammatical paradigms like verb conjugations. While Preoperational children "centrate" or focus on one attribute of an object, like its appearance, Concrete Operational children "decentrate," accommodating multiple attributes, and can perform and reverse mental operations. For example, a Preoperational child can count pennies, but not understand ten pennies spread into a long row equal ten pennies clustered together. Children in Concrete Operations, instead of focusing on appearance, will use logic and simply count the pennies, showing that each group has the same number regardless of how they look.

Conservation

Piaget identified conservation as a key ability, which Preoperational preschoolers have not yet developed. Piaget found elementary school-age Concrete Operational children develop conservation—the understanding that an object or substance conserves, or retains, its essential properties despite changes in appearance or configuration. For example, adults know a cup of liquid is the same amount regardless of the size or shape of the container

- 33 -

holding it. Preoperational children, seeing equal amounts of liquid poured from a tall thin glass to a short wide one or vice versa, will "centrate" (focus exclusively) on either height or width and say one glass holds more. Concrete operational children know logically that the amounts are equal regardless of container shape/appearance. When asked how they know, they use empirical evidence and logic: "Of course it's the same amount; I just saw you pour it from the tall glass to the short one." A universal phenomenon is that after developing conservation, we take it for granted and cannot remember or believe our earlier Preoperational thinking.

Erikson's developmental theory

Erikson's theory is based on Freud's, but focuses on psychosocial rather than psychosexual development. Erikson proposed infants are in his first stage, named for its nuclear conflict of Basic Trust vs. Mistrust. Erikson found if an infant's needs are met adequately and consistently, the baby will form a sense of trust in the world; but if they are not fully and/or regularly met, the baby will form a sense of mistrust in the environment and people. Erikson proposed a positive outcome for resolving the nuclear crisis in each stage; in this stage it is Hope. Caregivers understanding this theory and stage will feed a baby on a regular schedule and not leave the child crying from hunger for long times. They will change the baby's diaper timely when needed rather than letting him/her experience discomfort and cry too long. Moreover, caregivers will meet infant needs for interaction, especially holding and cuddling. Making care/nurturing predictable for babies establishes optimism. The negative outcome of Mistrust is linked to worthless feelings, even suicide.

Erikson's second stage of psychosocial development centers on the nuclear conflict of Autonomy vs. Shame and Doubt. Toddlers in this stage are engaged in learning to walk and toilet-training, involving motor control and self-control. They are also learning to assert themselves. This is one reason for tantrums characteristic of this age group. Toddlers who begin loudly saying "No!" are not merely obstinate or difficult, but are learning to express their wills. Erikson designated Will as the positive outcome of resolving the conflict in this stage, as well as self-control and courage. Children allowed to use their emerging skills to try things on their own become more independent, developing autonomy. Those not allowed to practice and progress in making choices and/or are made to feel ashamed during toilet-training/while learning other new skills, learn to doubt themselves and their abilities instead of developing independence. Adults appreciating this theory and stage let children express preferences and practice new skills, supplying needed encouragement, support, and positive reinforcement without overly restricting, controlling, or punishing them.

In his theory of psychosocial development, Erikson proposed his third stage revolves around the nuclear conflict of Initiative vs. Guilt. Erikson described 3- to 5-year-olds in this stage as being at the "play age." Having developed the ability for make-believe/pretend play, children imitate parents and other adults in their activities. At these ages, children begin taking the initiative to plan and enact scenarios wherein they play roles and use objects to symbolize other things. Through creating situations and stories, they experiment and identify socially with adult roles and behaviors. They are also more actively exploring their environments. Relationships expand from parents to family. The positive outcome/strength of this stage is Purpose. Children thwarted in fulfilling their natural goals and desires develop the negative outcome of Guilt through adults' punishing them for trying to control their environments and/or adults' controlling them too much. Adults understanding this encourage and support pretend play. They encourage and approve children for initiating activities rather than inhibiting or always directing their actions.

Erikson termed the fourth stage of his psychosocial theory of development as centering on the nuclear conflict of Industry vs. Inferiority. Children commonly enter this stage around the years beginning school, also coinciding with the close of the early childhood years. Children at elementary school ages acquire a great many new skills and much new knowledge. This enables them to attempt and accomplish many more things, which they are expected to do in school. Their increased ability and accomplishment engender a positive sense of Industry. Children's most important relationships are no longer only with their parents and family, but with friends, neighbors, classmates, teachers, and other school staff. Hence social interactions are central during this stage. Children feeling unequal to new tasks develop a sense of Inferiority compared to peers. Parents and educators who encourage and reinforce children's desires and attempts to learn and practice new skills and perform tasks help them develop senses of method and competence. Unsupportive/punitive adult responses result in restricted competencies and/or lack of motivation.

Bandura's Social Learning Theory

Psychologist Alfred Bandura developed the primary theory of social learning. While his theory incorporates elements of behaviorism in that environmental rewards and punishments that shape the behaviors and learning of children, Bandura focused more on the social dimension of learning in that he found the context of social interactions the most important medium and influence for learning. Bandura's theory also incorporates elements of cognitive theory by emphasizing the roles played by the cognitive processes of attention, memory, and motivation in learning. Bandura found children learn by observing and imitating the behaviors of models, including adults, older children, and peers. He proposed four conditions required for this learning: Attention, Retention, Reproduction, and Motivation. Adults understanding Bandura's theory realize children can learn new behaviors by seeing others be rewarded for performing these, and then imitating them; this greatly expands children's learning potential. Bandura also proved that children viewing violent video content engage in more aggressive behaviors, informing adults of the importance of monitoring and controlling children's exposure to media influences.

Hierarchy of needs in Maslow's humanistic theory of self-actualization

Maslow proposed humans are driven by needs, and meeting the most basic needs is prerequisite to meeting more advanced needs. Maslow's needs hierarchy is depicted as a pyramid, with the most fundamental needs at the base. Its five levels are (1) physiological needs: air, water, sleep, and food necessary for survival; (2) security needs: shelter and a safe environment; (3) social needs: feeling loved, receiving affection, and belonging to a family and/or group; (4) esteem needs: feeling personal value, accomplishment, and social recognition; and (5) self-actualizing needs: achieving optimal personal growth and realizing one's full potential. For example, babies and young children must have clean air to breathe and be fed and rested to survive before other needs can be addressed. Children must have safe places to live, then their needs for love and belonging can be met. Once a child feels loved and part of a family/group, s/he can develop self-esteem through accomplishments and feeling valued by society. After satisfying these, children can self-actualize.

Carl Rogers' theory

Rogers believed in actualization or realizing one's full potential as did fellow humanist Abraham Maslow. While Maslow applied self-actualization to humans, Rogers applied the "actualization tendency" to all life forms. Rogers gave the name "conditions of worth" to the process he observed whereby others give individuals things based not on need but worthiness. For example, while babies usually receive care based on need, as they grow older, adults establish conditions of worth: children get dessert if they finish dinner/vegetables; they get drinks or snacks after finishing a task/activity/lesson/class; and most significantly, they often get affection on condition of acceptable/desirable behavior. In behaviorism, this is called contingencies of reinforcement: rewards are given contingent on desired behaviors. Rogers would likely disagree with this practice, which he called conditional positive regard. He felt it makes children do what others want, not what they want or need, and teaches them conditional positive self-regard, i.e. self-esteem dependent on external standards. Rogers' remedy was unconditional positive regard—unconditional love and acceptance.

Rogers said all organisms naturally pursue a tendency to actualize or make the best of life. Organismic valuing is the natural tendency to value what is healthy, e.g. avoiding bad-tasting foods, which can be poisonous or rotten. Organismic valuing leads to positive regard/esteem, engendering positive self-regard/self-esteem, reflecting what Rogers called the real self—the person one becomes under optimal conditions. Rogers observed society substitutes conditions of worth for organismic valuing, giving us things based not on our needs but on meeting society's required conditions. Children are taught early they will receive something they want on the condition they do what adults want. This establishes conditional positive regard, meaning children only feel esteemed by others on others' conditions; this develops conditional positive self-regard, or self-esteem dependent on others' esteem. This creates an unattainable ideal self-based on others' standards rather than the real self. For Rogers, incongruence between real and ideal self-causes neurosis. Rogers' required qualities for effective therapists—congruence/genuineness, empathy, and respect—are equally effective in early childhood education.

Behaviorist or learning theory

Major principles of behaviorism include these: Organisms learn through interacting with the environment. Environmental influences shape behavior. Environmental stimuli elicit responses from organisms. Hypothetical constructs like the mind and/or inner physiological changes are unnecessary for scientifically describing behaviors—everything organisms do, including feeling and thinking. Learning and behavior change are achieved through arranging the learner's environment to elicit certain responses, increasing the probability of repeating those responses by rewarding them (positive reinforcement) and decreasing repetition of unwanted behaviors by punishing (positive punishment) or ignoring them (extinction). Just as Thorndike previously found all animals including humans learn the same way, Skinner also found his principles applied equally to rats, pigeons, and people. His methods have become so popular that early childhood educators routinely give positive reinforcement—verbal praise, treats, and privileges—for performing new skills and demonstrating socially desirable behaviors; teach young children complex tasks in steps (shaping/chaining/task analysis); take away privileges to punish unwanted behaviors (negative punishment); and remove aversive stimuli for complying (negative reinforcement).

Ivan Pavlov's experiments with dogs proved that when a stimulus evoking a reflexive response—drooling at the taste of meat—was repeatedly paired with an unrelated/"neutral" stimulus—a bell ringing—dogs came to associate the unrelated stimulus with the original response and drooled on hearing the bell without tasting meat. This proved generalizable to humans. Edward L. Thorndike's experiments with cats also applied to humans. Thorndike introduced the Law of Effect: we are more likely to repeat behaviors receiving desirable consequences. This set the stage for B. F. Skinner's later work. John B. Watson maintained that because inner states cannot be observed or measured, only observable outer behaviors should be used in psychology and learning. Skinner experimented with operant conditioning, wherein behaviors are trained and shaped through manipulating their antecedents/preceding stimuli and consequences/following stimuli. He expanded behaviorism into a comprehensive theory, including detailed rules for teaching new behaviors and modifying behavior (behavior modification).

Positive and negative reinforcement and positive and negative punishment

Behavioral techniques include positive reinforcement, introducing rewarding stimuli for emitting desired behaviors; negative reinforcement, removing unwanted stimuli for emitting desired behaviors; positive punishment, introducing aversive stimuli for unwanted behaviors; and negative punishment, removing desired stimuli for unwanted behaviors. Research has found positive reinforcement the most powerful of all these. One reason is that people are highly motivated by rewards. Another is that all behaviors meet needs; punishment suppresses certain behaviors, but then other behaviors must emerge to fill the same need. If a child misbehaves to get attention, even scolding/other punishment can constitute attention. But if rewarded for more appropriate behavior to get attention, like asking an available adult or peer for interaction, the child meets the attention need while replacing a maladaptive behavior with an adaptive one. Another reason is punishment's limitations: preschoolers may stop misbehaving after one teacher's punishment, but not with another teacher; punishment not applied consistently loses its effect. Also, punishment can cause resentment, anger, defiance, or fearfulness in young children.

In behaviorism, reinforcement means strengthening the probability a behavior will be repeated. Skinner used the terms positive vs. negative to mean introducing vs. removing, not good vs. bad. Therefore, positive reinforcement is introducing something rewarding immediately after a behavior. When a child's behavior is rewarded, s/he will repeat it to obtain repeated rewards: Johnny gets a treat or praise for putting away his toys; he will do it again. Negative reinforcement is rewarding by removing something unwanted: Johnny dislikes noisy crowds at preschool. One day he wakes up earlier, is taken to preschool earlier, finds it quieter and less crowded; he will want to get up and arrive earlier again. Positive punishment is introducing an aversive consequence for a behavior: Johnny refuses to put toys away; his parents then make him clean up the entire room; he is less likely to repeat the refusal. Negative punishment is removing a desirable stimulus: Johnny refuses to put away toys; his parents prohibit watching TV; he is less likely to keep refusing.

Teaching and Supporting Diverse Children

Characteristics of infants and young children with intellectual disabilities

Newborns with intellectual disabilities, especially of greater severity, may not demonstrate normal reflexes, such as rooting and sucking reflexes, necessary for nursing. They may not show other temporary infant reflexes such as the Moro, Babinski, swimming, stepping, or labyrinthine reflexes, or they may demonstrate weaker versions of some of these. In some babies, these reflexes will exist but persist past the age when they normally disappear. Babies with intellectual disabilities are likely to display developmental milestones at later-than-typical ages. The ages when they do display milestones vary according to the severity of the disability and by individual. Young children with intellectual disabilities are likely to walk, self-feed, and speak later than normally developing children. Those who learn to read and write do so at later ages. Children with mild intellectual disabilities may lack curiosity and have quiet demeanors; those with profound intellectual disabilities are likely to remain infantile in abilities and behaviors throughout life. Intellectually disabled children will score below normal on standardized IQ tests and adaptive behavior rating scales.

Infections that can cause intellectual disabilities
Congenital cytomegalovirus (CMV) is passed to fetuses from mothers, who may be asymptomatic. About 90% of newborns are also asymptomatic; 5% to 10% of these have later problems. Of the 10% born with symptoms, 90% will have later neurological abnormalities, including intellectual disabilities. Congenital rubella, or German measles, is also passed to fetuses from unvaccinated and exposed mothers, causing neurological damage including blindness or other eye disorders, deafness, heart defects, and intellectual disabilities. Congenital toxoplasmosis is passed to fetuses by infected mothers, who can be asymptomatic, with a parasite from raw or undercooked meat that causes intellectual disabilities, vision or hearing loss, and other conditions. Encephalitis is brain inflammation caused by infection, most often viral. Meningitis is inflammation of the meninges, or membranes, covering the brain and is caused by viral or bacterial infection; the bacterial form is more serious. Both encephalitis and meningitis can cause intellectual disabilities. Maternal human immunodeficiency virus (HIV) and acquired immunodeficiency syndrome (AIDS) can be passed to fetuses, destroying immunity to infections, which can cause intellectual disabilities. Maternal listeriosis, a bacterial infection from contaminated food, animals, soil, or water, can cause meningitis and intellectual disabilities in surviving fetuses and infants.

Environmental, nutritional, and metabolic influences
Environmental deprivation syndrome results when developing children are deprived of necessary environmental elements—physical, including adequate nourishment (malnutrition); climate or temperature control (extremes of heat or cold); hygiene, like changing and bathing; and so on. It also includes lack of adequate cognitive stimulation, which can stunt a child's intellectual development, and neglect in general. Malnutrition results from starvation; vitamin, mineral, or nutrient deficiency; deficiencies in digesting or absorbing foods; and some other medical conditions. Environmental radiation, depending on dosage and time of exposure, can cause intellectual disabilities. Congenital hypothyroidism (underactive thyroid) can cause intellectual disabilities, as can hypoglycemia (low blood sugar) from inadequately controlled diabetes or occurring independently and infant hyperbilirubinemia. Bilirubin, a waste product of old red blood

cells, is found in bile made by the liver and is normally removed by the liver; excessive bilirubin buildup in babies can cause intellectual disabilities. Reye syndrome, caused by aspirin given children with flu or chicken pox, or following these viruses or other upper respiratory infections, or from unknown causes, produces sudden liver and brain damage and can result in intellectual disabilities.

Genetic abnormalities affecting the nervous system

Rett syndrome is a nervous system disorder causing developmental regression, particularly severe in expressive language and hand function. It is associated with a defective protein gene on an X chromosome. Having two X chromosomes, females with the defect on one of them can survive; with only one X chromosome, males are either miscarried, stillborn, or die early in infancy. Rett syndrome produces many symptoms, including intellectual disabilities. Tay-Sachs disease, an autosomal recessive disorder, is a nervous system disease caused by a defective gene on chromosome 15 resulting in a missing protein for breaking down gangliosides, chemicals in nerve tissues that build up in cells, particularly brain neurons, causing damage. Tay-Sachs is more prevalent in Ashkenazi Jews. The adult form is rare; the infantile form is commonest, with nerve damage starting in utero. Many symptoms, including intellectual disabilities, appear at 3 to 6 months and death occurs by 4 to 5 years. Tuberous sclerosis, caused by genetic mutations, produces tumors damaging the kidneys, heart, skin, brain, and central nervous system. Symptoms include intellectual disabiltiies, seizures, and developmental delays.

Genetic or inherited metabolic disorders

Adrenoleukodystrophy is an X-linked genetic trait. Some female carriers have mild forms, but it affects more males more seriously. It impairs metabolism of very long-chain fatty acids, which build up in the nervous system (as well as adrenal glands and male testes). The childhood cerebral form, manifesting at ages 4 to 8, causes seizures, visual and hearing impairments, receptive aphasia, dysgraphia, dysphagia, intellectual disabilities, and other effects. Galactosemia is an inability to process galactose, a simple sugar in lactose, or milk sugar. By-product buildup damages the liver, kidneys, eyes, and brain. Hunter syndrome, Hurler syndrome, and Sanfilippo syndrome each cause the lack of different enzymes; all cause an inability to process mucopolysaccharides or glycosaminoglycans (long sugar-molecule chains). Hurler and Sanfilippo (but not Hunter) syndromes are autosomal recessive traits, meaning both parents must pass on the defect. All cause progressive intellectual disabilities. Lesch-Nyhan syndrome, affecting males, is a metabolic deficiency in processing purines. It causes hemiplegia, varying degrees of intellectual disabilities, and self-injurious behaviors. Phenylketonuria (PKU), an autosomal recessive trait, causes lack of the enzyme to process dietary phenylalanine, resulting in intellectual disabilities.

Prescription drugs, substances of abuse, and diseases in pregnant mothers

Warfarin, a prescription anticoagulant drug to thin the blood and prevent excessive clotting, can cause microcephaly (undersized head) and intellectual disabilities in an infant when the mother has taken it during pregnancy. The prescription antiseizure drug Trimethadione can cause developmental delays in babies when it has been taken by pregnant mothers. Maternal abuse of solvent chemicals during pregnancy can also cause microcephaly and intellectual disabilities. Maternal crack cocaine abuse during pregnancy can cause severe and profound intellectual disabilities and many other developmental defects in fetuses, which become evident when they are newborns. Maternal alcohol abuse can cause fetal alcohol syndrome, which often includes intellectual disabilities, among many other symptoms. Maternal rubella (German measles) virus can cause intellectual disabilities as well as visual and hearing impairments and heart defects. Maternal herpes simplex virus can cause microcephaly, intellectual disabilities, and microophthalmia (small or no eyes). The varicella (chicken pox) virus in pregnant mothers can also cause intellectual disabilities as well as muscle atrophy in babies.

Attachment styles identified by Mary Ainsworth

Mary Ainsworth worked with John Bowlby, discovering the first empirical evidence supporting his attachment theory. From her Strange Situation experiments, she identified secure, insecure and avoidant, insecure and resistant, and insecure and disorganized attachment styles. Securely attached children show normal separation anxiety when mother leaves and happiness when she returns, avoid strangers when alone but are friendly with mother present, and use mother as a safe base for environmental exploring. Insecure and resistant children show exaggerated separation anxiety, ambivalence and resistance to mother upon reuniting, fear strangers, cry more, and explore less than secure or avoidant babies. Insecure and avoidant children show no separation anxiety or stranger anxiety and little interest on reunions with mother and are comforted equally by mother or strangers. Insecure and disorganized types seem dazed and confused, respond inconsistently, and may mix resistant and ambivalent and avoidant behaviors. Secure styles are associated with sensitive, responsive caregiving and children's positive self-images and other images, resistant and ambivalent styles with inconsistent caregiving, and avoidant with unresponsive caregivers. Avoidant, resistant, and disorganized styles, associated with negative self-images and low self-esteem, are most predictive of emotional disturbances.

Learning disabilities (LDs) and their respective characteristics

Dyslexia, the most common LD, means deficiency or inability in reading. It primarily affects reading but can also interfere with writing and speaking. Characteristics include reversing letters and words, for example, confusing b and d in reading and writing; reading won as now, confusing similar speech sounds like /p/ and /b/, and perceiving spaces between words in the wrong places when reading. Dyscalculia is difficulty doing mathematical calculations; it can also affect using money and telling time. Dysgraphia means difficulties specifically with writing, including omitting words in writing sentences or leaving sentences unfinished, difficulty putting one's thoughts into writing, and poor handwriting. Central auditory processing disorder causes difficulty perceiving small differences in words despite normal hearing acuity; for example, couch and chair may be perceived as cow and hair. Background noise and information overloads exacerbate the effects. Visual processing disorders affect visual perception despite normal visual acuity, causing difficulty finding information in printed text or from maps, charts, pictures, graphs, and so on; synthesizing information from various sources into one place; and remembering directions to locations.

Variables having the potential to cause learning disabilities

LDs are basically neurological disorders. Though they are more specific to particular areas of learning than global disorders like intellectual disabilities, scientific research has found correlations between LDs and many of the same factors that cause intellectual disabilities, including prenatal influences like excessive alcohol or other drug consumption, diseases, and so on. Once babies are born, glandular disorders, brain injuries, exposure to secondhand smoke or other toxins, infections of the central nervous system, physical trauma, or malnutrition can cause neurological damage resulting in LDs. Hypoxia and anoxia (oxygen loss) before, during, or after birth is a cause, as are radiation and chemotherapy. These same influences often cause behavioral disorders as well as LDs. Another factor is genetic: Both LDs and behavior disorders have been observed to run in families. While research has not yet identified specific genetic factors, heritability does appear to be a component in influencing learning and behavioral disorders.

Neurological damage found in LD and ADHD children

Various neurological research studies have revealed that children diagnosed with LDs and ADHD have at least one of several kinds of structural damage to their brains. Scientists have found smaller numbers of cells in certain important regions of the brains of some children with learning and behavioral disorders. Some of these children are found to have brain cells of smaller than normal size. In some cases, dysplasia is discovered; that is, some brain cells migrate into the wrong area of the brain. In some children with learning and behavioral disorders, blood flow is found to be lower than normal to certain regions in the brain. Also, the brain cells of some children with learning and behavioral disabilities show lower levels of glucose metabolism; glucose (blood sugar) is the brain's main source of fuel, so inadequate utilization of glucose can affect the brain's ability to perform some functions related to cognitive processing, as in LDs, and to attention and impulse control, as in ADHD.

Anxiety disorders

Anxiety disorders include generalized anxiety disorder (GAD), obsessive-compulsive disorder (OCD), posttraumatic stress disorder (PTSD), panic disorder, social phobia, and specific phobias. All share a common characteristic of overwhelming, irrational, and unrealistic fears. GAD involves excessive worrying about anything or everything and free-floating anxiety. Anxiety may be about real issues but is nonetheless exaggerated and spreads, overtaking the child's life. OCD involves obsessive and preoccupied thoughts and compulsive or irresistible actions, including often bizarre rituals. Germ phobia, constant hand washing, repeatedly checking whether tasks are done or undone, and collecting things excessively are common. PTSD follows traumatic experiences/events. Children have frequent, extreme nightmares, crying, flashbacks wherein they vividly perceive or believe they are experiencing the traumatic event again, insomnia, depression, anxiety, and social withdrawal. Symptoms of panic disorder are panic attacks involving extreme fear and physical symptoms like a racing heart, cold hands and feet, pallor, hyperventilation, and feeling unable to move. Children with social phobia develop fear and avoidance of day care, preschool, or other social settings. Specific phobias are associated with specific objects, animals, or persons and are often triggered by traumatic experiences involving these.

Emotional disturbances

Researchers have investigated emotional disturbances but have not yet established known causes for any. Some disturbances, for example the major mental illness schizophrenia, seem to run in families and hence include a genetic component; childhood schizophrenia exists as a specific diagnosis. Factors contributing to emotional disturbances can be biological or environmental but more often are likely a combination of both. Dysfunctional family dynamics can often contribute to child emotional disorders. Physical and psychological stressors on children can also contribute to the development of emotional problems. Some people have attributed emotional disturbances to diet, and scientists have also researched this but have not discovered proof of cause and effect. Bipolar disorder is often successfully treated with the chemical lithium, which affects sodium flow through nerve cells, so chemical imbalance may be implicated as an etiology. Pediatric bipolar disorder, which has different symptoms than adult bipolar disorder, correlates highly with histories of bipolar and other mood disorders or alcoholism in both parents.

Pediatric bipolar disorder

Bipolar, formerly called manic-depressive disorder, has similar depressive symptoms in children as adults. However, children's mood swings often occur much faster, and children show more symptoms of anger and irritability than other adult manic symptoms. Bipolar children's most common symptoms include frequent mood swings; extreme irritability; protracted (up to several hours) tantrums or rages; separation anxiety; oppositional behavior; hyperactivity, impulsivity, and distractibility; restlessness and fidgetiness; silly, giddy, or goofy behavior; aggression; racing thoughts; grandiose beliefs or behaviors; risk-taking; depressed moods; lethargy; low self-esteem; social anxiety; hypersensitivity to environmental or emotional triggers; carbohydrate (sugar or starch) cravings; and trouble getting up in the morning. Other common symptoms include bed-wetting (especially in boys), night terrors, pressured or fast speech, obsessive or compulsive behaviors, motor and vocal tics, excessive daydreaming, poor short-term memory, poor organization, learning disabilities, morbid fascinations, hypersexuality, bossiness and manipulative behavior, lying, property destruction, paranoia, hallucinations, delusions, and suicidal ideations. Less common symptoms include migraines, bingeing, self-injurious behaviors, and animal cruelty.

Conduct disorder

Factors contributing to conduct disorders in children include genetic predispositions, neurological damage, child abuse, and other traumatic experiences. Children with conduct disorders display characteristic emotional and behavioral patterns. These include aggression: They bully or intimidate others, often start physical fights, will use dangerous objects as weapons, exhibit physical cruelty to animals or humans, and assault and steal from others. Deliberate property destruction is another characteristic—breaking things or setting fires. Young children are limited in some of these activities by their smaller size, lesser strength, and lack of access; however, they show the same types of behaviors against smaller, younger, weaker, or more vulnerable children and animals, along with oppositional and defiant behaviors against adults. Also, while truancy is impossible or unlikely in preschoolers, and running away from home is less likely, young children with conduct disorders are likely to demonstrate some forms of seriously violating rules, another symptom of this disorder.

Childhood-onset schizophrenia

The incidence of childhood-onset schizophrenia is rare, but it does exist. One example of differential diagnosis involves distinguishing qualitatively between true auditory hallucinations and young children's "hearing voices" otherwise: In the latter case, a child hears his or her own or a familiar adult's voice in his or her head and does not seem upset by it, while in the former, a child may hear other voices, seemingly in his or her ears, and is frightened and confused by them. Tantrums, defiance, aggression, and other acting-out, externalized behaviors are less frequent in childhood-onset schizophrenia than internalized developmental differences, for example, isolation, shyness, awkwardness, fickleness, strange facial expressions, mistrust, paranoia, anxiety, and depression. Children demonstrate nonpsychotic symptoms earlier than psychotic ones. However, it is difficult to use prepsychotic symptoms as predictors due to variance among developmental peculiarities. While psychiatrists find the course of childhood-onset schizophrenia somewhat more variable than in adults, child symptoms resemble adult symptoms. Childhood-onset schizophrenia is typically chronic and severe, responds less to medication, and has a more guarded prognosis than adolescent- or adult-onset schizophrenia.

Psychotic disorders

Psychosis is a general psychiatric category referring to thought disturbances or disorders. The most common symptoms are delusions that is, believing things that are not true, and hallucinations, that is, seeing, hearing, feeling, tasting, or smelling things that are not there. While early childhood psychosis is rarer than at later ages, psychiatrists confirm it does occur. Moreover, prognosis is poorer for psychosis with onset in early childhood than in adolescence or adulthood. Causes can be from known metabolic or brain disorders or unknown. Younger children are more vulnerable to environmental stressors. Also, in young children, thoughts distorted by fantasy can be from normal cognitive immaturity, due to lack of experience and a larger range of normal functioning, or pathology; where they lie on this continuum must be determined by clinicians. Believing one is a superhero who can fly can be vivid imagination or delusional; having imaginary friends can be pretend play or hallucinatory. Other developmental disorders can also cloud differential diagnosis.

Visual impairments

Historically, it was thought that VI children developed more slowly than normal; however, it is now known that ages for reaching developmental milestones are equally variable in VI babies as in others and that they acquire milestones within equal age ranges. One developmental difference is in sequence: VI children tend to utter their first words or subject-verb 2-word sentences earlier than other children. Some VI children also demonstrate higher levels of language development at younger-than-typical ages. For example, they may sing songs from memory or recall events from the past at earlier ages than other children. This is a logical development in children who must rely more on input to their hearing and other senses than to their vision when the latter is impaired. Totally blind babies reach for objects later, hence explore the environment later; hand use, eye-hand coordination, and gross and fine motor skills are delayed. Blind infants' posture control develops normally (rolling, sitting, all-fours, and standing), but mobility (raising on arms, pulling up, and walking) are delayed.

Visual impairments in babies and young children
Syndrome-related and other malformations like cleft iris or lens dislocation causing VI can have prenatal origins. Cataracts clouding the eye's lens can be congenital, traumatic, or due to maternal rubella. Eyes can be normal, but impairment in the brain's visual cortex can cause VI. Infantile glaucoma, like adult glaucoma, causes intraocular fluid buildup pressure and VI. Conjunctivitis and other infections cause VI. Strabismus and nystagmus are ocular-muscle conditions, respectively causing eye misalignments and involuntary eye movements. Trauma damaging the eyeball(s) is another VI cause. The optic nerve can suffer from atrophy (dysfunction) or hypoplasia, that is, developmental regression, usually prenatally

due to neurological trauma; acuity cannot be corrected. Refractive errors like nearsightedness, farsightedness, and astigmatism are correctable. Retinoblastoma, or behind-the-eye tumors, can cause blindness and fatality; surgical or chemotherapeutic treatment is usually required before age 2. Premature infants can have retinopathy of prematurity or retrolental fibroplasia. Cryotherapeutic treatment seems to stop disease progression. Its effects range from none to severe VI (approximately 25% of children) to complete blindness.

Blindness

Blind babies and children are more dependent than others on adults, affecting development. With control of their inner realities but not of their outer environments, blind children may withdraw, seeking and responding less to social interaction. They may not readily develop concepts of the external world or self-concepts as beings separate from the world and the understanding that they can be both agents and recipients of actions relative to the environment. Mother-infant smiling initiates recognition, attachment, and communication in sighted babies; blind infants smile on hearing mother's voice at 2 months. Only tactile stimuli like tickling and nuzzling evoke regular smiling in blind babies. Missing facial expressions and other visual cues, blind children have more complicated social interactions. They often do not understand the basics of playing with others and seem emotionally ambivalent or uninterested and uncommunicative. Peers may reject or avoid them; adults often overprotect them. Self-help skills like chewing, scooping, self-feeding, teeth brushing, grooming, and toilet training are delayed in blind children.

Impacts of blindness upon cognitive development

Blind children have more difficulty determining and confirming characteristics of things, hence defining concepts and organizing them into more abstract levels; their problem-solving is active but harder, and they construct different realities than sighted children. Blind babies typically acquire object permanence (the understanding that unseen objects still exists) a year later than normal; they learn to reach for objects only by hearing. Understanding cause-and-effect relationships is difficult without visual evidence. Blind babies and toddlers take longer to understand and object's constancy regardless of their orientation in space, affecting their ability to orient toys and their own hands. Blind children can identify object size differences and similarities, but classifying object differences and similarities in other attributes requires longer times and more exposures to various similar objects. Blind children's development of the abilities to conserve object properties like material or substance, weight, amount and volume, length, and liquid volume is later than normal.

Speech and language impairments

In speech, most phonological disorders are articulatory; that is, children fail to pronounce specific speech sounds or phonemes correctly beyond the normal developmental age for achieving accuracy. Stuttering, disfluency, and rate and rhythm disorders cause children to repeat phonemes, especially initial word sounds; to repeat words; to prolong vowels or consonants; or to block, that is, straining so hard to produce a sound that, pressure builds, but no sound issues. Their speech rates may also speed and slow irregularly. Children with voice disorders can have voices that sound hoarse, raspy, overly nasal, higher- or lower-pitched than normal, overly weak or strident, and whispery or harsh. Hoarseness is common with vocal nodules and polyps. Cleft palate commonly causes hypernasality. In language, one of the most common impairments is delayed language development due to

- 44 -

environmental deprivation, intellectual disabilities, neurological damage or defects, hearing loss, visual impairment, and so on. Children with neurological damage or disorders may exhibit aphasias, language disorders characterized by receptive difficulty with understanding spoken or written language, or expressive difficulty constructing spoken or written language.

Factors that can contribute to speech and language impairments

Some speech and language disorders in children have unknown causes. Others have known causes such as hearing loss: Speech and language are normally acquired primarily through the auditory sense, so children with impaired hearing have delayed and impaired development of speech and language. Brain injuries, neurological disorders, viral diseases, and some medications can also cause problems with developing language or speech. Children with intellectual disabilities are more likely to have delayed language development, and their speech is also more likely to develop more slowly and to be distorted. Cerebral palsy causes neuromuscular weakness and incoordination of speech. When severe, it can cause inability to produce recognizable speech sounds; some children without speech can still vocalize, and some cannot. A cleft palate or lip and other physical impairments affect speech. Inadequate speech-language modeling at home inhibits speech-language development. Vocal abuse in children (screaming, coughing, throat clearing, or excessive talking) can cause vocal nodules or polyps, causing voice disorders. Stuttering can be related to maturation, anxiety or stress, auditory feedback defects, or unknown causes.

Hearing impairments

Half or more (50% to 60%) of infant hearing losses have genetic origins—Down and other genetically based syndromes or the existence of parental hearing loss. About 25% or more of infant hearing losses are caused by maternal infections during pregnancy, such as cytomegalovirus (CMV), postnatal complications like blood transfusions or infection with meningitis, or traumatic head injuries. Included in this 25% or more are babies having nongenetic neurological disorders or conditions that affect their hearing. Malformations of the ears, head, or face can cause hearing loss in babies. Babies spending 5 days or longer in neonatal intensive care units (NICUs) or having complications while in the NICU are also more likely to suffer hearing loss. Around 25% of babies are diagnosed with hearing loss whose etiology is unknown.

Signs of hearing impairments

If an infant does not display a startle response at loud noises, this is a potential sign of hearing loss. This can also indicate other developmental disabilities, but because hearing loss is the most prevalent disability among newborns, hearing screening is a priority. Between birth and 3 or 4 months old, babies should turn toward the source of a sound; if they do not, it could indicate hearing loss. A child who does not utter first words like mama or dada by age 1 could have hearing impairment. When babies or young children do not turn their heads when their names are called, adults may mistake this for inattention or ignoring; however, children turning upon seeing adults, but not upon hearing their names, can indicate hearing loss. Babies and children who seem to hear certain sounds but not others may have partial hearing losses. Delayed speech-language development or unclear speech, not following directions, saying "Huh?" often, and wanting higher TV or music volumes can indicate hearing loss in children.

Physical and health impairments

In the special education field of early childhood education, other health impairment is a term referring to health and physical conditions that rob a child of strength, vitality, or alertness or that cause excessive alertness to environmental stimuli, all having the end result of impeding the child's ability to attend or respond to the educational environment. Health problems can be acute, that is short-term or temporary but serious, or chronic, that is, long-term, persistent, or recurrent. Some examples of such health and physical impairments include: cerebral palsy, spina bifida, amputations or missing limbs, muscular dystrophy, cystic fibrosis, asthma, rheumatic fever, sickle-cell anemia, nephritis or kidney disease, leukemia, Tourette syndrome, hemophilia, diabetes, heart disease, AIDS, and lead poisoning. All these conditions and others can interfere with a child's development and ability to attend and learn. In addition to seizure disorders, which often cause neurological damage, seizure-controlling medications also frequently cause drowsiness, interfering with attention and cognition. Attention deficit and attention deficit hyperactivity disorders (ADD and ADHD) limit attention span, focus, and concentration and thus are sometimes classified as health impairments requiring special education services.

Characteristics of babies and children with physical and health impairments
The characteristics of children having various physical or health impairments can range from having no limitations to severe limitations in their activities. Children with cerebral palsy, for example, usually have deficiencies in gross and fine motor development and deficits in speech-language development. Physical and health conditions causing severe debilitation in some children not only seriously limit their daily activities but also cause multiple primary disabilities and impair their intellectual functioning. Other children with physical or health impairments function at average, above-average, or gifted intellectual and academic levels. An important consideration when working with babies and young children having physical or health impairments is handling and positioning them physically. Correctly picking up, holding, carrying, giving assistance, and physically supporting younger children and arranging play materials for them based on their impairment is not only important for preventing injury, pain, and discomfort; it also enables them to receive instruction better and to manipulate materials and perform most efficiently. Preschoolers with physical impairments also tend to have difficulty with communication skills, so educators should give particular attention to facilitating and developing these.

Developmental delays

Developmental delays can come from genetic or environmental causes or both. Infants and young children with intellectual disabilities are most likely to exhibit developmental delays. Their development generally proceeds similarly to that of normal children but at slower rates; milestones are manifested at later-than-typical ages. Sensory impairments such as with hearing and vision can also delay many aspects of children's development. Children with physical and health impairments are likely to exhibit delays in their motor development and performance of physical activities. Another factor is environmental: Children deprived of adequate environmental stimulation commonly show delays in cognitive, speech-language, and emotional and social development. Children with autism spectrum disorders often have markedly delayed language and speech development; many are nonverbal. Autistic children also typically have impaired social development, caused by and inability or difficulty with understanding others' emotional and social nonverbal communications. When they cannot interpret these, they do not know how to respond and also cannot imitate them; however, they can often learn these skills with special instruction.

Characteristics in infants and young children that can indicate developmental delays
Developmental delays mean that a child does not reach developmental milestones at the expected ages. For example, if most babies normally learn to walk between 12 and 15 months of age, a 20-month-old who is not beginning to walk is considered as having a developmental delay. Delays can occur in cognitive, speech-language, social-emotional, gross motor skill, or fine motor skill development. Signs of delayed motor development include stiff or rigid limbs, floppy or limp body posture for the child's age, using one side of the body more than the other, and clumsiness unusual for the child's age. Behavioral signs of children's developmental delays include inattention, or shorter than normal attention span for the age; avoiding or infrequent eye contact; focusing on unusual objects for long times or preferring objects over social interaction; excessive frustration when attempting tasks normally simple for children their age; unusual stubbornness; aggressive and acting-out behaviors; daily violent behaviors; rocking; excessive talking to oneself; and not soliciting love or approval from parents.

IDEA's legal definition of traumatic brain injury

TBI is defined by the IDEA law (the Individuals with Disabilities Education Act) as "an acquired injury to the brain from external physical force, resulting in total or partial functional disability or psychosocial impairment, or both, that adversely affect a child's educational performance." This definition excludes injuries from birth trauma, congenital injuries, and degenerative conditions. TBI is the foremost cause of death and disability in children (and teens) in the USA. The most common causes of TBI in children include falls, motor vehicle accidents, and physical abuse. In spite of the IDEA's definition, aneurysms and strokes are examples of internal traumas that can also cause TBI in babies and young children. External head injuries that can result in TBI include both open and closed head injuries. Shaken baby syndrome is caused by forcibly shaking an infant. This causes the brain literally to bounce against the insides of the skull, causing rebound injuries, resulting in TBI and even death.

Characteristics traumatic brain injuries
TBI can impair a child's cognitive development and processing. It can impede the language development of children, which is dependent upon cognitive development. Children who have sustained TBI often have difficulties with attention, retention and memory; reasoning, judgment, understanding abstract concepts and thinking abstractly, and problem-solving abilities. TBIs can also impair a child's motor functions and physical abilities. The sensory and perceptual functions of children with TBI can be abnormal. Their ability to process information is often compromised. Their speech can also be affected. In addition, TBIs can impair a child's psychosocial behaviors. Memory deficits are commonest, tend to be more long lasting, and are often area specific; for example, a child may recall personal experiences but not factual information. Other common characteristics of TBI include cognitive inflexibility or rigidity, damaged conceptualization and reasoning, language loss or poor verbal fluency, problems with paying attention and concentrating, inadequate problem solving, and problems with reading and writing.

Multiple disabilities

The term multiple disabilities refers to any combination of more than one disabling condition. For example, a child may be both blind and deaf due to causes such as having rheumatic fever in infancy or early childhood. Anything causing neurological damage before, during, or shortly after birth can result in multiple disabilities, particularly if it is widespread rather than localized. For example, infants deprived of oxygen or suffering traumatic brain injuries in utero, during labor or delivery, or postnatally can sustain severe brain damage. So can babies having encephalitis or meningitis and those whose mothers abused drugs prenatally. Infants with this type of extensive damage can often present with multiple disabilities, including intellectual disabilities, cerebral palsy, physical paralysis, mobility impairment, visual impairment, hearing impairment, and speech-language disorders. They may have any combination of or all of these disabilities as well as others. In addition to a difficulty or inability with normal physical performance, multiply disabled children often have difficulty acquiring and retaining cognitive skills and transferring or generalizing skills among settings and situations.

Prematurity or preterm birth

Babies born before 37 weeks' gestation are classified as premature or preterm. Premature infants can have difficulty with breathing, as their lungs are not fully developed, and with regulating their body temperatures. Premature infants may be born with pneumonia, respiratory distress, extra air or bleeding in the lungs, jaundice, sepsis or infection, hypoglycemia (low blood sugar), severe intestinal inflammation, bleeding into the brain or white-matter brain damage, or anemia. They have lower-than-normal birth weights, body fat, muscle tone, and activity. Additional typical characteristics of premature infants include apnea (interrupted breathing); lanugo (a coating of body hair that full-term infants no longer have); thin, smooth, shiny, translucent skin through which veins are visible; soft, flexible ear cartilage; cryptorchidism (undescended testicles) and small, non-ridged scrotums in males; enlarged clitorises in females; and feeding difficulties caused by weak or defective sucking reflexes or incoordination of swallowing with breathing.

Disabling conditions that can result from premature births
Physicians find it impossible to predict the long-term results of prematurity for any individual baby based on an infant's gestational age and birth weight. However, some related immediate and long-term effects can be identified. Generally, the lower the birth weight and the more prematurely a child is born, the greater the risk is for complications. Infants born at less than 34 weeks of gestation typically cannot coordinate their sucking and swallowing and may temporarily need feeding or breathing tubes or oxygen. They also need special nursery care until able to maintain their body temperatures and weights. Long-term complications of prematurity can include bronchopulmonary dysplasia, a chronic lung condition; delayed physical growth and development; delayed cognitive development; mental or physical delays or disabilities; and blindness, vision loss, or retinopathy of prematurity (formerly called retrolental fibroplasia). While some premature infants sustain long-term disabilities, some severe, other babies born prematurely grow up to show no effects at all; and any results within this range can also occur.

Screening young children for developmental disorders

If a child's development is suspected of being delayed—for example, the child is not reaching developmental milestones during expected age ranges—a developmental screening may be administered. Screening tests are quickly performed and yield more general results. The hospital or doctor's office may give a questionnaire to the parent or caregiver to complete for a screening. Alternatively, a health or education professional may administer a screening test to the child. Screening tests are not intended to diagnose specific conditions or give details; they are meant to identify children who may have some problem. Screenings can overidentify or under-identify developmental delays in children. Hence, if the screening identifies a child as having developmental delay(s), the child is then referred for a developmental evaluation—a much longer, more thorough, comprehensive, in-depth assessment using multiple tests, administered by a psychologist or other highly-trained professional. Evaluation provides a profile of a child's strengths and weaknesses in all developmental domains. Determination of needs for early intervention services or treatment plans is based on evaluation results.

If a young child has been screened for developmental disorders or delays within the past 6 months and no changes have been observed or reported, repeat screening may be waived. Initial screenings are required. Hearing and vision screenings are mandatory in screening young children. Formal developmental measures are also required, which may include screening tests of motor skills development, cognitive development, social-emotional development, and self-help skills development. Formal screening tests of speech-language development are also required. Additional tests recommended during screening include informal measures. For example, checklists, rating scales, and inventories may be used to screen a child's behavior, mood, and performance of motor skills, cognitive skills, self-help skills, and social and emotional skills. On checklists, parents or caregivers check whether the child does or does not demonstrate listed behaviors, or assessors may complete them via parent or caregiver interviews or interviewing and observing the child. Rating scales ask parents, caregivers, and assessors to rate a child's behaviors, affect, mood, and so on, within a range of numbered and labeled descriptions. Inventories list demonstrated skills and needs. Behavioral observations and existing records and information are also used.

Collaborative approaches
Historically, the tradition was to conduct kindergarten screenings of children entering schools around age 5. However, in recent years, school districts have developed community referral networks to assist in the processes of Child Find, screening, evaluation, and referral for early intervention and early childhood special education and related services. Current models are more informal, proactive, and collaborative. Cooperative educational interagency service efforts give parents information about normal early childhood development and available community resources and offer opportunities for developmental screenings of their young children. Specific procedures are governed by individual U.S. state laws. Generally, district networks implementing current models send developmental review forms to parents to complete in advance, and then they attend a developmental screening at a community site. Parents discuss normal early childhood growth and development with program staff, while in the same room, trained professionals observe their children as they play. Children's vision and hearing are also screened. Parents can discuss their children's current development with psychologists, early childhood educators, or counselors. Thereafter, they can learn about community resources.

Data that a developmental evaluation of a young child needs to incorporate

The child's social history should be obtained. This is typically done by a social worker. Details of the child's developmental progress heretofore; the family's composition, socioeconomic status, and situation; and the child's and family's health and medical histories and status should be emphasized. A physician's or nurse's medical assessment is required, including a physical examination, and if indicated, a specialist's examination. A psychologist typically assesses intellectual and cognitive development; at least one such test is generally required. At least one test of adaptive behavior is also required to assess emotional-social development. Self-help skills are evaluated; this may be included within cognitive, adaptive behavior, or programming assessments. Communication skills are typically evaluated by a speech-language pathologist. Both receptive and expressive language must be tested and comprehensively rather than simply by single-word vocabulary tests. As indicated, speech articulation is also tested. At least one test of motor skills, typically administered by a physical or occupational therapist, is required. Programming evaluation requires at least one criterion-referenced or curriculum-based measure, typically administered by an educator.

Behavioral variations and characteristics of ADHD

While the chief symptoms associated with ADHD are inattentiveness, impulsive behavior, distractibility, and excessive physical activity, there is considerable variation among individual children having ADHD. For example, the degree of severity of this condition can vary widely from one child to the next. In addition, each child can vary in how much he or she exhibits each of these primary characteristics. Some children might not appear to behave very impulsively but show severe deficits in attention. Some may focus better, but only for short periods, and are very easily distracted. Some display very disruptive behavior, while others do not but may daydream excessively, not attending to programming. In general, children who have ADHD can show deficits in following rules and directions. Also, when their developmental skills are evaluated or observed, they are likely to demonstrate inconsistencies in performance over time. To identify or select specific intervention methods and strategies, professionals should use a comprehensive evaluation to obtain information about the child's specific behaviors in his or her natural environment that need remediation.

Child Find process

Child Find is an ongoing process with the aim of locating, identifying, and referring young children with disabilities and their families as early as possible for service programs. This process consists of activities designed to raise public awareness and screenings and evaluations to identify and diagnose disabilities. The federal IDEA law mandates under Part B that disabled children are guaranteed early childhood special education services and under Part C that infants and toddlers at risk for developmental delays are guaranteed early intervention programs. (Eligibility guidelines vary by U.S. states.) The IDEA requires school districts to find, identify, and evaluate children with disabilities in their attendance areas. School districts have facilitated this Child Find process by establishing community informed referral networks whose members refer children who may have exceptional educational needs (EENs). Network members typically include parents, doctors, birth-to-3 programs, child care programs, Head Start programs, public health agencies, social service agencies, and any other community members with whom the young children come into contact.

Single and multiple risk factors in infants and toddlers

Scientists find that developmental outcomes for children are not reliably predicted by any one risk factor or event. Developmental risk increases with increased biological, medical, or

- 50 -

environmental risk factors. However, researchers have found some variables that afford resiliency in children to offset risk factors. These can include the child's basic temperament, the child having high self-esteem, the child having a good emotional relationship with at least one parent; and the child having experiences of successful learning. These findings indicate that assessments should include criteria for multiple biological and environmental risk factors, for cumulative biological and environmental risk factors, and for protective or resilience factors, considering all of these in the context of change occurring over time. Under the IDEA (the Individuals with Disabilities Education Act), U.S. states have the option to provide early intervention services to children considered at risk for adverse developmental outcomes as well as those already identified with them. Some states apply multiple-risk models, requiring three to five risk factors for service eligibility. Some states also determine eligibility with less DD when biological, medical, or environmental risk factors also exist.

Determining IDEA eligibility in infants and toddlers

The IDEA Part C specifies the areas of development that states must include in defining developmental delays. However, individual states must identify the criteria they use to determine eligibility, including pertinent diagnostic instruments, procedures, and functional levels. States currently use quantitative and qualitative measures. Quantitative criteria for developmental delay include: difference between chronological age and performance level, expressed as a percentage of chronological age; performance at a given number of months below chronological age; or number of standard deviations (SDs) below mean of performance on a norm-referenced test. Qualitative criteria include: development considered atypical or delayed for established norms or observed behaviors considered atypical. At least one state differentially defines delay according to a child's age in months, with the rationale that a 25% delay, for example, is very different for a 1-year-old than a 3-year-old. Quantitative criteria for defining delay and determining eligibility vary widely among states. A 25% or 20% delay; 2 SDs below mean in 1+ areas or 1.5 SD below mean in 2+ areas are some common state criteria.

Sources of information

Military families stationed both in the United States and overseas who have young special needs children can seek information and assistance from the federally funded organization Specialized Training of Military Families (STOMP). The staff of STOMP is composed of parents having special needs children themselves, who also have been trained to work with other parents of special needs children. STOMP staff members are spouses of military personnel who thus understand the unique, specialized circumstances and needs of military families. Another government agency, the U.S. Department of Defense, includes the office of the Department of Defense Education Activity (DoDEA) and provides comprehensive guidance to military families with special needs children who are eligible to receive, or are receiving, free appropriate public education (FAPE) as mandated by the IDEA law (the Individuals with Disabilities Education Act), whether that education is located in the United States or in other countries.

Evaluation of a preschool child aged 3 to 5 years
Under the IDEA (the Individuals with Disabilities Education Act), evaluation information sources include: physicians' reports, the child's medical history, developmental test results, current classroom observations and assessments (when applicable), completed

developmental and behavioral checklists, feedback and observations from parents and all other members of the evaluation team, and any other significant records, reports, and observations regarding the child. Under the IDEA, involved in the evaluation are parents, at least one regular education teacher and special education teacher if the child has these, and any special education service provider working with the child—for children receiving early intervention services from birth through age 2 and transitioning to preschool special education, it may be an early intervention service provider; a school administrator knowledgeable about children with disabilities, special education policies, regular education curriculum, and resources available; a psychologist or educator who can interpret evaluation results and discuss indicated instruction; individuals with special expertise or knowledge regarding the child (recruited by school or parents); when appropriate, the child; and other professionals, for example, physical or occupational therapists, speech therapists, medical specialists, and so on.

Providing special education services

If parents observe that their preschooler is not attaining developmental milestones within the expected age ranges or does not seem to be developing in the same way as most other children, they should seek evaluation for possible developmental delay or disability. Although 3- to-5-year-olds are likely not in elementary school yet, the elementary school in a family's school district is still the best first contact because the IDEA law (the Individuals with Disabilities Education Act) specifies that school districts must provide special education services at no family cost to eligible children, including preschoolers. Another excellent source of more information about special education is the National Dissemination Center for Children with Disabilities (NICHCY) of the U.S. Department of Education's Office of Special Education Programs. They partner with nonprofit organizations like the Academy for Educational Development (AED) to produce useful documents for families with special needs children. NICHCY supplies state resource sheets listing main contacts regarding special education services in each U.S. state. Families can obtain these sheets at NICHCY's website or by telephone.

Special education for preschoolers is education specifically designed to meet the individual needs of a child aged 3 to 5 years with a disability or developmental delay. The specialized design of this instruction can include adaptations to the content, to the teaching methods, and the way instruction is delivered to meet a disabled child's unique needs. Special education for preschoolers includes various settings, such as in the home, in classrooms, hospitals, institutions, and others. It also includes a range of related services, such as speech-language pathology services, specialized physical education instruction, early vocational training, and training in travel skills. The school district's special education system provides evaluation and services to eligible preschoolers free of charge. Evaluation's purposes are to determine whether a child has a disability under the IDEA's (the Individuals with Disabilities Education Act) definitions and determine that child's present educational needs.

After the evaluation of a preschool child

After a preschool child is evaluated, the parents and involved school personnel meet to discuss the evaluation results. Parents are included in the group that decides whether the child is eligible for special education services based on those results. For eligible children, the parents and school personnel will develop an IEP. Every child who will receive special education services must have an IEP. The main purposes of the IEP are (1) to establish reasonable educational goals for the individual child and (2) to indicate what services the school district will provide to the child. The IEP includes a statement of the child's present levels of functioning and performance. It also includes a list of more general instructional goals for the child to achieve through school and parental support along with more specific learning objectives reflecting those goals and specifying exactly what the child will be able to demonstrate, under what circumstances, how much of the time—for example, a percentage of recorded instances—and within what time period (e.g., 1 year).

Individualized Education Program

Individualized Education Program goals and objectives

In an IEP, the goals are more global, describing a skill for the child to acquire or a task to master. The objectives are more specific articulations of achievements that will demonstrate the child's mastery of the goal. For example, if a goal is for the child to increase his or her functional communicative vocabulary, a related objective might be for the child to acquire X number of new words in X length of time; another related objective could be for the child to use the words acquired in 90% of recorded relevant situations. If the goal is for the child to demonstrate knowledge and discrimination of colors, one objective might be for the child to identify correctly a red, yellow, and blue block 95% of the time when asked to point out each color within a group of blocks. Progress toward or achievement of some objectives may be measured via formal tests; with preschoolers, many others are measured via observational data collection.

Procedures and considerations to progress monitoring, updating, and revising IEPs

Once a child has been identified with a disability, determined eligible for special education and related services under the IDEA (the Individuals with Disabilities Education Act), and had an IEP developed and implemented, the child's progress must be monitored. Monitoring methods may be related to evaluation methods. For example, if a child identified with problem behaviors was initially evaluated using a behavioral checklist, school personnel can use the same checklist periodically, comparing its results to the baseline levels of frequency and severity originally obtained. If an affective disorder or disturbance was identified and instruments like the Beck Depression Inventory or Anxiety Inventory were used, these can be used again periodically; reduced symptoms would indicate progress. If progress with IEP goals and objectives is less or greater than expected, the IEP team meets and may revise the program. This can include specifying shorter or longer times to achieve some goals and objectives; lowering or raising requirements proving too difficult or easy; resetting successive objective criteria in smaller or larger increments; changing teaching methods, content, or materials used, and so on.

Legislation affecting the education of children with and without disabilities

The 1990 Individuals with Disabilities Education Act (IDEA) was reauthorized in 1997 and numbered Public Law 108-446. It provided more access for children with disabilities to the general education curriculum and extended collaborative opportunities for teachers, other professionals, and families of children with disabilities. No Child Left Behind (NCLB, 2001), the reauthorization of the Elementary and Secondary Education Act (ESEA), stressed accountability for outcomes by identifying schools and districts needing improvement and assuring teacher quality. It required school performance data to include disabled students' standardized test scores. NCLB emphasized giving teachers and administrators better research information and schools more resources, parents more information about their children's progress and the school's performance, and more local flexibility and control in utilizing federal education funds and in improving teacher qualifications, for example, through alternative certifications. And, 2004's IDEA reauthorization, Individuals with Disabilities Education Improvement Act (IDEIA), covers better alignment of NCLB with IDEA, appropriately identifying students needing special education, ensuring reasonable discipline while protecting special needs students defining highly qualified teachers, reducing paperwork, and increasing cooperation to decrease litigation.

IDEA law (the Individuals with Disabilities Education Act)

Public Law 94-142, the Education for All Handicapped Children Act/Education for the Handicapped Act (EHA), passed in 1975; and Public Law 99-457, the EHA Amendments, passed in 1986, provided foundations that were expanded by new 1990 legislation. As a result, EHA was renamed the Individuals with Disabilities Education Act (IDEA). The IDEA's six main principles follow:

(1) Publicly funded education cannot exclude any student because of the student's disability.
(2) The rights of students with disabilities and of their parents are assured by the protection of due process procedures.
(3) The parents of students with disabilities are encouraged to participate in their children's educations.
(4) The assessment of all students must be fair and unbiased.
(5) All students must be given a free, appropriate public education (FAPE), and it must be provided in the least restrictive environment (LRE) where the student and other students can learn and succeed.
(6) Information related to students with disabilities and their families must be kept confidential.

Section 504, Education for the Handicapped Act (EHA), EHA amendments, and ADA

In 1973, Section 504 of the Rehabilitation Act, also called Public Law 93-112, was enacted to ensure individuals with disabilities equal access to federally financed programs and to promote their participation in them. A child must have a physical or mental impairment that substantially limits a major life activity to be eligible for a free, appropriate public education (FAPE) under Section 504. This law stimulated motivation to educate students with disabilities, contributing to the passage of the Education for All Handicapped Children Act, also called Public Law 94-142, in 1975. This law provides that all children with disabilities must receive a FAPE provided in the least restrictive environment possible and individualized. Its procedural safeguards mandate due process. The 1986's EHA amendments, or Public Law 99-457 extended special education to disabled preschoolers aged 3 to 5 years; services to infants and toddlers are at each U.S. state's discretion. And 1990's Americans with Disabilities Act (ADA) requires access for disabled people to public buildings and facilities, transportation, and communication but does not cover educational services.

Recent legal changes to the Americans with Disabilities Act (ADA)

The ADA Amendments Act (ADAAA, 2009) overrules prior Supreme Court decisions narrowly interpreting the ADA. This qualifies many more conditions as disabilities.

(1) Physical or mental impairments substantially limiting one or more life activities now include immune system functioning; normal cell growth; brain, and neurological, respiratory, circulatory, endocrine, reproductive, digestive, bowel, and bladder functions, added to the existing activities of eating, sleeping, thinking, communicating, concentrating, lifting, and bending.

(2) Impairments include physical (deaf, blind, or wheelchair-bound); conditions (AIDS, diabetes, or epilepsy); mental illnesses and ADHD; record of impairment, for example, cancer in remission and regarded as impaired.

(3) Reasonable accommodations mean adaptations or modifications enabling persons with disabilities to have equal opportunities. The ADA describes this regarding equal employment opportunities, but it could also be interpreted relative to equal educational opportunities.

(4) Reasonable accommodations that would cause undue hardship, for example, financial, are not required.

- 55 -

Creating a Developmentally Appropriate Learning Environment

Genetic and environmental influences

Young children are subject to both genetic and environmental influences upon their relative risk of displaying antisocial behaviors. Research into factors influencing early childhood behavior identifies both genetic variables and environmental ones, like corporal punishment, affecting young children's propensities toward antisocial behavior. Children experiencing more corporal punishment display greater behavior problems; children at greater genetic risk also do. However, boys at higher genetic risk for behavior problems who also experience more corporal punishment exhibit the most antisocial behavior. Therefore, both genetic risk factors and corporal punishment significantly predict preschoolers' antisocial behavior. Additionally, the nature-nurture interaction of genetic risk factors and environmental punishment is statistically significant for young boys but not young girls. Such evidence shows that environmental learning is not wholly responsible for antisocial behavior: genetic variables predispose some young children to antisocial behaviors more than others.

Research-supported observations about genetic and biological influences

Adopted children with one or both biological parents having histories of alcohol abuse, criminal records, and/or major psychiatric illness are at double the risk for drug abuse as those having biological parents without such histories. While this risk is genetic, differential environmental influences can exacerbate or mitigate children's biological risk for engaging in addictive behaviors. For example, adopted children who experience difficulties in their adopted families, such as deaths or divorce, are at higher risk of developing drug abuse problems. Conversely, children whose biological parents' histories put them at higher genetic risk for abusing drugs—but who were adopted into loving, stable families—are less at risk for developing addictions. Researchers conclude that children with higher genetic risks for addiction are more vulnerable to adverse environmental influences in their adopted families than children with lower genetic risks. Also, genetic risks become less powerful in adoptive families having lower environmental risk factors.

Maturational factors

Many physiological factors affect the development of babies and young children. These dictate which kinds of learning activities are appropriate or ineffective for certain ages. For example, providing a newborn with visual stimuli from several feet away is wasted, as newborns cannot yet focus on distant objects. Adults cannot expect infants younger than about 5 months to sit up unsupported, as they have not yet developed the strength for it. Adults cannot expect toddlers who have not yet attained stable walking gaits to hop or balance upon one foot successfully. It is not coincidental that first grade begins at around 6 years: younger children cannot physically sit still for long periods and have not developed long enough attention spans to prevent distraction. This is also why kindergarten classes feature varieties of shorter term activities and more physical movement. Younger children also have not yet developed the self-regulation to keep from shouting out on impulse, getting up and running around, etc.—behaviors disruptive to formal schooling but developmentally normal.

Birth order

Neo-Freudian psychologist Alfred Adler proposed that a child's birth order relative to other children in a family is associated with corresponding influences on the child's personality and behaviors. For example, Adler found that the only child is regarded as a miracle of birth by parents with no prior experience of having a baby. This child receives the undivided attention of both parents, who may be overprotective of the child and/or spoil him/her. Some general characteristics of only children include preferring adults' company, using adult language, enjoying being the center of attention from adults, and finding it difficult to share with other children. Adler said the oldest/older child has been "dethroned"/displaced by a younger sibling and must learn to share. Parents often have very high expectations of the oldest/older child, give him/her much responsibility, and expect him/her to set an example for younger siblings. Older/oldest children may turn to fathers once a sibling is born. They may feel entitled to power, developing strict/authoritarian attitudes/behaviors. Given encouragement, they can develop helpful attitudes/behaviors.

In his psychoanalytic theory, Alfred Adler included birth order as one family influence on child personality development. For example, he found that the youngest child in a family, like an only child, is never "dethroned" or displaced by a new sibling. However, unlike an only child, the youngest sibling has many "parents" in the form of older siblings who help to raise, instruct, and influence him/her. Youngest siblings are often spoiled by the attentions of parents plus older siblings. Some youngest children continue to feel and behave like the "baby" of the family indefinitely. Many youngest children, always being littlest, wish to be bigger than siblings. As they grow, youngest siblings may make grandiose plans that never succeed. Adler found with twins, one is usually more active or stronger, and is often perceived by the parents as older—s/he may have been born a minute earlier and/or they perceive him/her as more mature. The stronger twin may develop as the leader; the other may develop problems with identity.

Psychoanalyst and theorist Adler included birth order as one factor in his study of influences on personality development. He identified general tendencies associated with each family birth position. For example, the second-born child was described by Adler as having a "pacemaker" in that there is always an older sibling ahead of this child. Adler found that the results of this position include the child's becoming more competitive out of attempts to overtake the elder sibling. He noted that competition could devolve into sibling rivalry. A second child might develop into a rebellious sort or might develop a habit of always trying to "top" or exceed everybody else's accomplishments. Adler described the middle child in a family as being "sandwiched" between older and younger siblings, so that s/he can feel "squeezed out" of any privileged or significant position. Some middle children may grow up to fight against injustice or unfairness; others may encounter difficulty establishing places for themselves. Some middle children develop even-tempered dispositions, with no extreme opinions and "take-it-or-leave-it" attitudes.

Adlerian psychoanalytic theory includes family birth order as an influence on personality development and behavior. For example, Adler described a child who is born after an older child has died as having a "ghost" ahead of him/her. Such a child, called a "ghost child," is likely to be subject to overprotection by the mother, who fears losing him/her after losing a child previously. The child may respond to parental overprotectiveness by taking advantage of the parent to get what s/he wants. Alternatively, some "ghost" children resent feeling parental comparisons to the deceased child, whose memory parents have idealized; in this case, the child may rebel. Adler said adoptive parents can be so grateful to have a child and so anxious to make up for the child's loss of biological parents, that they may spoil him/her; thus, the adopted child is more liable to develop very demanding, spoiled behaviors. The adopted child may ultimately either resent his/her biological parents for rejecting/leaving him/her or idealize them, negatively comparing the adoptive parents.

Adler found that the ways children are perceived and treated by parents and siblings relative to their birth order contribute to their personality formation and behavior. For example, Adler stated the only boy with girl siblings, surrounded by females when the father is not there, can develop either of opposite extremes: he may engage excessively in behaviors to prove he is the "man of the family" or develop effeminate behaviors through identifying with surrounding females. Adler found when a child is the only girl among male siblings, her older brothers can behave protectively toward her. An only girl among boys may make efforts to please the father and develop either of two opposing extremes: becoming a tomboy to compete with brothers or developing very feminine behaviors to differentiate from them. In families with all-male or all-female children, Adler noted parents who wanted a child of the other sex might dress one child as the opposite sex. The child may either exploit this role reassignment or strongly object to it.

Murray Bowen's Family Systems Theory

Dr. Bowen identified four basic family relationship patterns within what he called the Nuclear Family Emotional System. These patterns dictate where problems develop when the family system is under tension. Bowen labeled these patterns Marital Conflict; Dysfunction in One Spouse; Impairment of One or More Children; and Emotional Distance, which latter is associated with the first three. In Impairment of One or More Children, the parents focus their anxieties on one or more of their children. Their perception of the child(ren) is either negative or idealized. The more the parents focus on one child, the more that child reciprocally focuses on them, becoming more reactive to parental expectations, needs, and attitudes than siblings are. This process undermines the child's differentiation of self, a key factor in healthy individual development according to Bowen. The child becomes more susceptible to internalizing or externalizing family tensions, affecting his/her social relationships, school performance, and physical and mental health.

Family Projection Process

In the Family Projection Process, Dr. Murray Bowen found that parents can project their anxieties onto their children. When parents worry overly that something is wrong with one child, they may see everything the child does as proof of that worry. Their excessive efforts to remedy the child's "problem" can actually cause the child to develop the problem in reality, as the child's self-image becomes aligned with parental perceptions. While parents with such worries usually feel guilty of not giving the "problem" child enough attention, they have in fact directed more attention to this child than his/her siblings. Bowen found that children less engaged in this process have more realistic, mature relationships with parents and develop into more goal-oriented, less reactive, and less emotionally needy individuals. Both parents participate equally in the process in different ways; both are insecure relative to the child, but Bowen said typically one parent pretends to feel secure with the other's complicity.

In his theory, Bowen referred to the way parents transmit their emotional issues to children as the Family Projection Process, which involves three steps: (1) A parent focuses on a child, fearing something is wrong with that child. (2) The parent perceives the child's behavior as confirmation of this fear. (3) The parent then treats the child as though something really is wrong. When parents try to "fix" what they perceive is a problem in the child, their perception can become a self-fulfilling prophecy as the child eventually embodies that perception. For example, if parents perceive a child as helpless and are always helping her excessively, the child's self-image comes to mirror the parents' perception; the child becomes de facto helpless and dependent even though she may not have been so initially. The more intense this process is, the greater relationship sensitivities children develop, beyond those of their parents.

Nutrition

Raw or lightly steamed vegetables are best because excess heat destroys nutrients and frying adds fat calories. Fresh, in-season and flash-frozen fruits are more nutritious/less processed than canned. Adults should monitor young children's diets to limit highly processed produce, which can have excessive sugar, salt, or preservatives. Good protein sources include legumes, nuts, lean poultry, and fish. Adults should take care with young children to avoid choking hazards by cutting foods into bite-sized pieces. Serving nut butters instead of whole nuts is safer, but spread thinly on whole-grain breads/crackers or vegetable pieces, because young children can choke on large globs of nut butter as well. Omega-3 fatty acids from salmon, mackerel, herring, flaxseeds, and walnuts control inflammation, prevent heart arrhythmias, and lower blood pressure. Monounsaturated fats from avocados, olives, peanuts, their oils, and canola oil prevent heart disease, lower bad cholesterol, and raise good cholesterol. Polyunsaturated fats from nuts, seeds, and corn, soy, sesame, sunflower, and safflower oils lower cholesterol. These fats/oils should be served in moderation, avoiding saturated fats.

Babies are typically nourished via mother's milk or infant formula, and then with baby food; however, young children mostly eat the same foods as adults by the age of 2 years. Though they eat smaller quantities, young children have similar nutritional needs to those of adults. Calcium can be more important in early childhood to support the rapid bone growth occurring during this period; young children should receive 2–3 servings of dairy products and/or other calcium-rich foods. For all ages, whole-grain foods are nutritionally superior for their fiber and nutrients than refined flours, which have had these removed. Refined flours provide "empty calories" causing wider blood-sugar fluctuations and insulin resistance—Type 2 diabetes risks—than whole grains, which stabilize blood sugar and offer more naturally occurring vitamins and minerals. Darkly and brightly colored produce are most nutritious. Adults should cut foods into small, bite-sized pieces to prevent choking in young children, who have not yet perfected their biting, chewing, and swallowing skills.

Young children have smaller stomachs than adults and cannot eat as much at one time as teens or adults. However, it is common practice for today's restaurants to provide oversized portions. The historical tradition of encouraging young children to "clean their plates" is ill-advised considering these excessive portions and the abundance of food in America today. Adults can help young children by teaching them instead to respond to their own bodies' signals and eat only until they are satisfied. Adults can also place smaller portions of food on young children's plates and request to-go containers at restaurants to take leftovers home. Because young children cannot eat a lot at once, they must maintain their blood sugar and energy throughout the day by snacking between meals. However, "snack foods" need not be high in sugar, salt, and unhealthy fats. Cut pieces of fresh fruits and vegetables, whole-grain crackers and low-fat cheeses, and portable yogurt tubes make good snacks for young children.

<u>Unhealthy fats, hydration, sugar drinks, fruit juices, and portion sizes</u>
Saturated fats from meats and full-fat dairy should be limited; they can cause health problems like high cholesterol, cardiovascular disease, obesity, and diabetes. Trans fats are produced chemically by hydrogenating normally liquid unsaturated fats and converting them to solid, saturated fats as in margarine and shortening used in many baked goods. These are considered even unhealthier than regular saturated fats and should be avoided. (The words "partially hydrogenated" in the ingredients signal trans fats.) Infants derive enough water from mother's milk/formula, but young children should be given plenty of water and/or milk in "sippy cups" to stay hydrated. The common practice of giving young children fruit juice should be avoided. Even without added sugars, fruit juices crowd out room in small stomachs for food nutrients and cause dental cavities and weaken permanent teeth before they erupt. Children can also gain weight, as juice calories do not replace food calories the way actual fruit does with its fiber and solids. Young children should eat two-thirds of adult-sized portions.

Feeding strategies

Early childhood is an age range often associated with "finicky" eaters. Adults can experiment by substituting different foods that are similar sources of protein or other nutrients to foods young children dislike. Preparing meals to look like happy faces, animals, or have appealing designs can entice young children to eat varied foods. Engaging children age-appropriately in selecting and preparing meals with supervision can also motivate them to consume foods when they have participated in their preparation. Adults should model healthy eating habits for young children, who imitate admired adults' behaviors. Early childhood is when children form basic food-related attitudes and habits and so is an important time for influencing these. Children are exposed to unhealthy foods in advertising, at school, in restaurants, and with friends, so adult modeling and guidance regarding healthy choices are important to counteract these influences. However, adults should also impart the message early that no foods are "bad"/forbidden, allowing some occasional indulgences in small amounts, to prevent the development of eating disorders.

Sleep

Sleep allows the body to become repaired and recharged for the day and is vital for young children's growth and development. Children aged 2–5 years generally need 10–12 hours of sleep daily. Children 5–7 years old typically need 9–11 hours of sleep. Their sleep schedules should be fairly regular. While occasionally staying up later or missing naps for special events is not serious, overall inconsistent/disorganized schedules cause lost sleep and lethargic and/or cranky children. Some young children sleep fewer hours at night but need long daytime naps, while others need longer, uninterrupted nighttime sleep but seldom nap. Young children are busy exploring and discovering new things; they have a lot of energy and are often excited even when tired. Because they have not developed much self-regulation, they need adult guidance to calm down enough to go to sleep and will often resist bedtimes. Adults should plan bedtime routines. These can vary, but their most important aspect is consistency. Children then expect routines' familiar steps, and anticipating these comfort them.

The majority of early childhood experts think young children should not have adults in their rooms every night while they fall asleep. They believe this can interfere with young children's capacity for "self-soothing" and falling asleep on their own, making them dependent on an adult presence to fall asleep. Parents/caregivers are advised to help children relax until sleepy, and then leave, saying "Good night" and "I love you." Young children frequently feel more comfortable going to bed with a favorite blanket or stuffed animal and/or a night light. Regardless, fears and nightmares are still fairly common in early childhood. "Family beds," i.e. children sleeping in the same bed or adjacent beds with parents, are subject to controversy. However, this is traditional in many developing countries and was historically so in America. Whatever the individual family choice, it should be consistent as young children will be frustrated by inconsistent practices and less likely to develop good sleeping habits.

Relationship of sleep quality to blood sugar control in children with Type 1 (juvenile) diabetes
Researchers find blood sugar stability problematic for many children with Type 1 (juvenile) diabetes, despite all efforts by parents and children to follow diabetic health care rules, because of sleep differences. Diabetic children spend more time in lighter than deeper stages of sleep compared to nondiabetic children. This results in higher levels of blood sugar and poorer school performance. Lighter sleep and resulting daytime sleepiness tend to increase blood sugar levels. Sleep apnea is a sleep disorder that causes a person's breathing to be interrupted often during sleeping. These breathing interruptions result in poorer sleep quality, fatigue, and daytime sleepiness. Sleep apnea has previously been associated with Type 2 diabetes—historically adult-onset, though now children are developing it, too. It is now known that apnea is also associated with Type 1 diabetes in children: roughly one-third of diabetic children studied have sleep apnea, regardless of their weight (being overweight can contribute to apnea). Sleep apnea is additionally associated with much higher blood sugars in diabetic children.

Bedtime routines
Bedtime routines serve as transitions from young children's exciting, adventurous daytime activities to the tranquility needed for healthful rest. Adults should begin routines by establishing and enforcing a rule that daytime activities like rough-and-tumble physical play or TV watching stop at a specific time. While preschoolers may be less interested in computer/video games than older children, establishing limits early will help parents enforce stopping these activities at bedtime when they are older, too. Bath time is one good way to begin bedtime routines. Toys and games make baths fun, and bath washes with lavender and other soothing ingredients are now available to relax young children. Also, since young children eat smaller meals, healthy bedtime snacks are important. Too much/too little food will disrupt sleep, and too much liquid can cause bedwetting. Adults should plan nighttime snacks appropriately for the individual child. Bedtime reading promotes interest in books and learning, adult-child/family bonding, and calms children. Singing lullabies, hugging, and cuddling also support bonding, relax children, and make them feel safe and secure.

<u>Transitioning from sleeping in cribs to regular beds</u>
One of young children's significant transitions from infancy is moving from a crib to a "big bed." Some become very motivated to escape cribs. For example, some bright, adventurous toddlers and even babies have untied padded crib bumpers, stacked them, and climbed out of the crib. For such children, injury is a greater danger from a crib than a bed. Others, whose cognitive and verbal skills are more developed than motor skills, may stand/jump up and down, repeatedly calling, "Hey, I'm up!" until a parent comes. These children should be moved to regular beds, with guardrails and/or body pillows to prevent rolling/falling-out accidents. If a child is moved to a bed to free the crib for a new baby, this should be done weeks ahead of the infant's arrival if possible, to separate these two significant life events. Most young children are excited about "grown-up" beds. Some, if hesitant, can sleep in the crib and nap in the bed for a gradual transition until ready for the bed full-time.

Hygiene

<u>Dental hygiene</u>
Even while young children still have their deciduous/"baby" teeth, dental hygiene practices can affect their permanent/adult teeth before they erupt. For example, excessive sugar can weaken adult teeth before they even appear above the gumline. Adults should not only teach young children how important it is to brush their teeth twice and floss once daily at a minimum; moreover, they should model these behaviors. Children are far more likely to imitate parents' dental hygiene practices than do what parents only tell them but do not do themselves. Integrating tooth brushing into morning and bedtime routines promotes the habit. Adults can help motivate resistant children with entertaining toothbrushes that play music, spin, light up, and/or have cartoon illustrations. Young children have not developed the fine motor skills sufficient for flossing independently and will need adult supervision until they are older. Individual flossers are easier for them to use with help than traditional string dental floss.

<u>Hand-washing</u>
A major change during early childhood is that hygiene transforms from something adults do for children to something children learn to do themselves. Toddlers are typically learning toilet-training, getting many germs on their hands. Preschoolers today are also often exposed to germs in daycare or school settings. Adults must explain to young children using concrete, easily understood terms how germs spread; how hand-washing removes germs; and when and how to wash their hands. Adults also need to remind children frequently to wash their hands until it becomes a habit. Remind them hand-washing is required before eating, after toileting, after being outdoors, after sneezing/coughing, and after playing with pets. Because young children have short attention spans and can be impatient, they are unlikely to wash long or thoroughly enough. Adults can encourage this by teaching children to sing "Happy Birthday" or other 15- to 20-second songs/verses while washing, both assuring optimal hand-washing duration and making the process more fun.

<u>Bathing</u>
While infants are bathed by adults, by the time they are toddlers or preschoolers, they generally have learned to sit in a bathtub and wash themselves. However, regardless of their ability to bathe, young children should never be left unsupervised by adults in the bath. Young children can drown very quickly, even in an inch of water; an adult should always be in the bathroom. Also, adults should not let young children run bathwater: they are likely to make it too cold or hot. Adults can prevent scalding accidents by turning down

- 62 -

the water heater temperature. The adult should adjust water temperature and test it on his/her own inner arm (an area with more sensitive skin). Parents/caregivers should choose baby shampoos, soaps, and washes that do not irritate young eyes or skin, and keep adult bath products out of children's reach and sight. Very active children may need to bathe daily; others suffering dry, itchy skin should bathe every other day and/or have parents/caregivers apply mild moisturizing lotion.

Exercise

Young children need daily physical exercise to strengthen their bones, lungs, hearts, and other muscles. Throwing, catching, running, jumping, kicking, and swinging actions develop young children's gross motor skills. Children sleep better with regular physical activity and are at less risk for obesity. Playing actively with other children also develops social skills, including empathy, sharing, cooperation, and communication. Family playtimes strengthen bonding and let parents model positive exercise habits. Outdoor play is fun for youngsters; running and laughing lift children's moods. Pride at physical attainments moreover boosts children's self-images and self-esteem. At least 60 minutes of physical activity most days is recommended for children. This includes jungle gyms, slides, swings, and other playground equipment; family walks, bike-riding, playing backyard catch, baseball, football, or basketball; adult-supervised races or obstacle courses; and age-appropriate community sports activities/leagues. Adults should plan and supervise activities to prevent injuries. They should also provide repeated sunscreen applications for outdoor activities to prevent sunburn and long-term skin damage.

Physical activities for winter months and/or inclement weather
While summer is typically the season of the most physical activity as it allows outdoor activities and the greatest choice of activities, adults can also provide many opportunities for young children to enjoy and benefit from exercise in winter and bad weather. Many young children like participating (at their own levels) in their parents' workouts to exercise videos. Adults can arrange "dance parties" in the living room for young children on cold/rainy days. Current video games, like Dance Dance Revolution, promote physical movement to music, making it fun while developing attention, cognitive processing, coordination, timing, and footwork. Parents can enroll their young children in indoor dance, gymnastics, karate, swimming, or ice-skating lessons and/or help them join indoor basketball, soccer, ice hockey, volleyball, or other sports teams. Families can attend local ice-skating rinks or bowling alleys for recreation. Many community facilities offer discounted fees, scholarships, or even free programs for families with financial considerations. Some companies also offer employees' families access to recreational centers/activities.

Exposure to TV and other media

Preschool-aged children are not yet cognitively able to distinguish between reality and fantasy. Therefore, overly violent or intense content in TV or other media can frighten them. Additionally, exposure to video violence has been proven to increase aggressive behaviors in young children. Moreover, using TV as a babysitter for long times excludes more cognitively stimulating and interactive pursuits. Parents/caregivers can provide young children with paints, crayons, and modeling clay. They can play board games and simple card games, do puzzles, sing songs, and read stories with young children. Pretend/make-believe play develops during early childhood, so adults can encourage their playing "house,"

- 63 -

"dress-up," or "auto shop." Park/playground trips afford outdoor play and physical activity/exercise. Visiting local museums, zoos, or planetariums combine education and entertainment with outings. In multiple-child families, it is important for each child to get some one on one time with parents regularly, even in unstructured activities like going to the hardware store with Daddy or keeping Mommy company while she washes dishes.

Cultures and cultural values

The culture in a society influences, even determines, our individual values, as do both historical and current social and political occurrences. Our values then influence the ways in which children are valued and raised. As American educators, we can understand the "American" perspective on early childhood better through understanding cultural diversity. We tend to fixate on our own culture's beliefs of truth as the only existing reality, but depending on our personal histories and values and current conditions, there can actually be multiple right ways of doing things. For example, Western cultures value children's early attainment of independence and individuality, but Eastern cultures value interdependence and group harmony more than individualism. In affluent societies, letting children explore the environment early and freely is valued, but in poor and/or developing societies, parents protect children, keeping them close and even carrying them while working, and thus do not value early freedom and exploration.

Individualistic vs. collectivistic cultures

Anthropologists have classified various world cultures along a continuum of how individualistic or interdependent their structures and values are. Investigating these differences is found to afford much insight and application for early childhood education. The predominant culture in America is considered very individualistic. Children are encouraged to assert themselves and make their own choices to realize their highest potentials, with the ultimate goal of individual self-fulfillment. Collectivistic/sociocentric cultures, however, place the highest importance on group well-being; if collective harmony is disrupted by individual assertiveness, such self-assertion is devalued. Some educators characterize this contrast as the difference between standing out (individualist) and fitting in (collectivist). Researchers note that when asked to finish "I am…" statements, members of interdependent cultures tend to supply a family role, religion, or organization (e.g. "a father/a Buddhist"); whereas members of individualistic cultures cite personal qualities (e.g. "intelligent/hardworking"). Research finds American culture most individualistic, Latin American and Asian cultures most interdependent, and European cultures in the middle.

Age, ethnicity, and income

Research traces many variations in well-being and health to early childhood. These differences come from inequities in service access and treatment, congenital health problems, and early exposure to greater familial and community risk factors. Child groups at risk that are overrepresented in our population include young children, low-income children, and minority children. More young children than older children are likely to live in economically disadvantaged families. As of 2005, more than 10 million children aged 0–5 years lived in the U.S. 20 percent of these were in families classified as poor, i.e. with income below the federal poverty level (FPL), and 42 percent were in families designated low-income, i.e. with income below double the FPL. Of more than 2 million American children aged 0–5 living in families identified as extremely poor, i.e. with income less than half the

FPL, minority groups were also overrepresented. The younger the children are, the greater the adverse effects of poverty are on their developmental outcomes.

Racial and ethnic origin

Children are at higher risk for inadequate development when they are born prematurely or with low birth weights. Recent research found racial and ethnic disparities in these birth conditions. For example, rates of low birth weights in 2004 were almost double for African-Americans as for whites (13.4 percent versus 7.1 percent). Latinos had similar but slightly lower risk than whites for low birth weight (6.9 percent versus 7.1 percent). Native American/Alaska Natives had slightly higher risk than white (7.5 percent versus 7.1 percent), as did Asian/Pacific Islanders (7.9 percent versus 7.1 percent). In oral health, 28 percent of preschoolers have had tooth decay. Moreover, data show that in children aged 2–5 years, oral disease increased 15.2 percent from 1994–2002, equaling 600,000 more children. It was found 13.9 percent of children aged 2–5 years were overweight or obese. Risk for overweight/obesity is higher for low-income and minority children. These groups are also at higher risk for poorer quality and continuity in asthma treatment. Asthma's prevalence as well as asthma-related morbidity and deaths are higher in African-American children than white children.

Proportionately more mothers in minority and low-income groups—up to 40 percent—suffer maternal depression than in other parts of the population. Maternal depression is associated with poor mother-child bonding; lower child scores in language and reading; and higher prevalence of depression and other mental health problems later in children. Low-income and minority families are at higher risk for developmental difficulties and mental health issues. According to U.S. surveys, about one-third or over 3 million of young children have two or more health and developmental risk factors. These risk factors include maternal mental health, maternal education, family poverty, and race/ethnicity. Each added risk factor increases the probability of either greater developmental risk or worse health status. Risk increases exponentially with multiple factors. One risk factor doubles risk; two factors more than triple it; three causes almost five times the risk; and four risk factors represent 14 times the risk of developmental delay or poor health.

Relationship of environment, social and emotional support, self-image, and success

Researchers have recently found that a child's sense of self is significant in predicting success in life. Even when a child's family environment involves multiple stressors, having a good relationship with one parent mitigates a child's psychosocial risks. As a child grows older, a close, supportive, lasting relationship with an adult outside the family can confer similar protection. Such relationships promote self-esteem in a child. Children with positive self-esteem are more able to develop feelings of control, mastery, and self-efficacy to achieve tasks, and they are more able to manage stressful life experiences. Such children demonstrate more initiative in forming relationships and accomplishing tasks. They reciprocally derive more positive experiences from their environments. Children with positive self-concepts pursue, develop, and sustain experiences and relationships that support success. Their positive self-images are further enhanced by these successes, generating additional supportive relationships and experiences. While we often hear about negative cycles of poverty, abuse, or failure, positive cycles of success can be equally as self-perpetuating.

Economically deprived and culturally diverse environments

Historically, disadvantages of poverty have been the focus of research; e.g. lack of toys, inadequate verbal interactions limiting visual discrimination and linguistic development or risk factors like less education, poorer nutrition, family stressors, medical illness, inadequate social stimulation, and insufficient social-service support leading to school dropouts, delinquency, unemployment, and perpetuated poverty. However, more recent research also identifies poverty's advantages, including opportunities for young children to play with peers and older children with little adult intervention, promoting empathy, cooperation, self-control, self-reliance, and sense of belonging; experience with multiple teaching styles, especially modeling, observation, and imitation; and language acquisition within a culturally-specific context through rich cultural traditions of stories, songs, games, and toys. These findings illuminate the resiliency or stress resistance of some children. Recent research also identifies protective factors against risk factors. These protections contribute to child resiliency, including the child's personality traits; having stable, supportive, cohesive family units; and having external support systems promoting positive values and coping skills.

Effects of racial, ethnic, and economic disparities

Parenting, home safety, and school readiness
According to the National Survey on Early Childhood Health, significant differences are reported in Latino and African-Americans' parenting practices, home routines, and home safety measures. These differences are associated with differing degrees of positive early childhood development. Research studies have also revealed that American children in minority groups, on the average, demonstrate lower school readiness levels when they begin formal education than white American children do. The research furthermore shows that most of these differences in school readiness levels are associated with differences in family income. Researchers also comment that disparities among racial and ethnic groups in their school readiness and subsequent academic achievement in school may be additional contributors to discrimination against minority racial and ethnic groups by teachers and other educational personnel.

Health care aspects of immunizations, regular providers, and satisfaction
Although the disparity in childhood immunizations between white and minority infants and toddlers has decreased, still, fewer minority children are receiving standard immunizations than white children in America. For example, the preschool rates for receiving each major vaccination from 2003–2004 in America were the lowest among non-Latino black, Native American, and Alaskan Native children. One sign of health service quality and continuity is having a regular health care provider. Recent national surveys have found that while more than 80 percent of children under the age of 5 in economically affluent families are seen at physicians' offices or HMOs for care when sick, not much more than 54 percent of children under age 5 in economically poor families are seen for sick care. The National Survey of Early Childhood Health has found African-American and Latino parents report more dissatisfaction with pediatricians and more unmet needs for early childhood development services than white parents. Twice as many Latino as white parents felt providers never or only occasionally understood their individual child's needs.

Differing socioeconomic and racial effects on mental, emotional, and social health

According to the National Survey of Child and Adolescent Well-Being, in recent years over 40 percent of toddlers and over 68 percent of preschoolers who were in contact with the child welfare system had high levels of need, developmentally and behaviorally. But overall, fewer than 23 percent of these children were getting services to address these needs. Thus, young children of socioeconomically disadvantaged families were found to have more developmental and behavioral problems than children in other socioeconomic groups, yet were also less likely to receive help with such problems. Another social and emotional difference related to racial group membership has been reflected by levels of violence in the family. 2003 data found that over 15 percent of African-American families experienced violent conflicts, compared to below 9 percent of white families and over 11 percent of Latino families. Racial groups classified as "other" constituted over 12 percent. Experts concede that styles of disagreeing can be influenced by cultural and demographic variables. However, they find the strongest influence on conflicts becoming violent to be parental stress.

Inequity in health insurance coverage for children of minority groups

Research has demonstrated that after taking health insurance status into account, there are no significant socioeconomic differences in how family organization and doctor/health care practitioner visits are related. Furthermore, research has shown that having health insurance coverage decreases differences in developmental and health outcomes for young children. However, despite these findings, children of minority groups are less likely than their nonminority peers to have either private or public health care coverage. Regarding access to health care services, it has been found that parents whose first language was not English were only half as likely to get preventive health care for their infants as native English-speaking families. This inequity in service delivery was found to be constant across white, African-American, and Latino families that had infants, but not in Asian-American families having infants.

Unequal health care treatment of young minority children in America

According to data collected by the National Survey of Early Childhood Health, minority families have less communication and guidance from pediatric health care providers than white families. For example, African-American parents were found to make significantly fewer phone calls than white parents to pediatric health care practices. Latino parents made fewer than half the calls that white parents did; African-American parents made fewer than three-fourths of the calls white parents did. This survey also found that pediatricians and other pediatric health care service providers were more likely to emphasize topics of household alcohol and drug use and community violence when they talked with minority patient families than they did in discussions with white patient families. African-American children are found far more likely to have special health care needs than white children; yet researchers find that even after controlling for health status, insurance, and other pertinent variables, health care providers are still nearly twice as likely not to refer minority children to specialists and consultants.

Leveling inequalities in early childhood care, health, and education

Eliminating unequal treatment in early childhood has significant benefits, including lowering overall national rates of poverty; improving overall health and education measures; saving long-term health care costs; decreasing disabilities; and lengthening lives by decreasing mortality rates. The effects of low income and racism on young children and their families are complex, and these influences interact with one another. Therefore it is impossible or extremely difficult to solve problems generated by one of these social factors without including the other associated influencing factors. Because of the interrelationships of variables, strategies on a system level have the most potential for effectiveness. For example, job training and placement programs that could help parents economically are limited in effectiveness if quality child care is not also available to those parents. Enhancing educational programs could improve academic performance, but not if young students are too hungry to benefit from instruction. And the measurement and monitoring of developmental, health, and educational outcomes will not change their disparity unless treatment inequities are resolved.

Early Childhood Comprehensive Systems (ECCS)

According to the National Center for Children in Poverty, Early Childhood Comprehensive Systems (ECCS) initiatives in each U.S. state have the ability to further methods that can decrease socioeconomically related health care inequities in early childhood, which generates positive impacts for the rest of children's lives. To raise and shape consciousness of health care issues affected by income and race, experts recommend that ECCS establish connections between projects/programs designed to eradicate poverty and racism and efforts in developing early childhood systems. Another consciousness-raising strategy recommended for ECCS is to work at increasing the general public's awareness of racial, ethnic, and economic disparities in early childhood health care and to work at increasing such awareness in health professionals, educators, early care providers, and other significant stakeholders who regularly provide services to young children. ECCS can also include racial/ethnic data in performance monitoring; encourage state SCHIP and Medicaid agencies to do the same; analyze state data for disparities in risk, access, and outcomes, including small-area analyses, geocoding, etc.; and identify and measure unequal treatment through data analysis.

Experts in early childhood development find that state ECCS should target their support toward communities with larger populations of minority and low-income families. Inasmuch as local systems have limited resources, some state ECCS might need to allocate more of these resources to communities having higher risks of adverse outcomes for children. ECCS can also provide assistance to communities by helping them assess their local assets, strengths, needs, and risk factors. Early childhood development experts emphasize that state ECCS should focus their efforts on improving the quality of health care services that are available within communities where all or the majority of residents are members of minority groups and/or have low socioeconomic status. Another way in which state ECCS can strengthen the supports available in communities for citizens who are subject to unequal health care treatment according to their demographic groups is to offer and provide incentives for community development projects that are designed to decrease health care treatment disparities based on racial/ethnic and economic differences.

Early childhood experts advise that each U.S. state's ECCS should implement strategies designed to monitor health care providers and services for cultural and linguistic competency, and to improve these competencies. One example of such improvement is ensuring that specific training in cultural and linguistic competency and cross-cultural competency is integrated into the training of both health care providers and early childhood educators. ECCS can also be responsible for seeing that parent education materials and resources in health care are translated into the native languages of local families who are not native English speakers, and supporting interpreter and translator services for communities having families needing these. Experts find that ECCS can additionally improve child and family health services by supporting various early childhood service settings in employing nonprofessional/community health workers. Moreover, ECCS can help further equality and consistency of health care across varied demographic groups by applying research evidence-based guidelines regarding health care, family support, early learning, and related services and programs.

Zone of Proximal Development (ZPD)

Vygotsky identified an area or range of skills wherein a learner can complete a task s/he could not yet complete independently, given some help. He termed this area the Zone of Proximal Development. Vygotsky found if a child is given assistance, guidance, or support from someone who knows more—especially another child just slightly more advanced in knowledge and/or skills—the first child can not only succeed at a task s/he is still unable to do alone; but that child also learns best through accomplishing something just slightly beyond his/her limits of expertise to do alone. Jerome Bruner coined the term "scaffolding" to describe temporary support that others give learners for achieving tasks. Scaffolding is closely related to the ZPD in that only the amount of support needed is given, and it allows the learner to accomplish things s/he could not complete autonomously. Scaffolding is gradually withdrawn as the child's skills develop, until the child reaches the level of expertise needed to complete the task on his/her own.

Montessori Method

Maria Montessori's method emphasizes children's engagement in self-directed activities, with teachers using clinical observations to act as children's guides. In introducing and teaching concepts, the Montessori Method also employs self-correcting ("autodidactic") equipment. This method focuses on the significance and interrelatedness of all life forms, and the need for every individual to find his/her place in the world and to find meaningful work. Children in Montessori schools learn complex math skills and gain knowledge about diverse cultures and languages. Montessori philosophy puts emphasis on adapting learning environments to individual children's developmental levels. The Montessori Method also believes in teaching both practical skills and abstract concepts through the medium of physical activities. Montessori teachers observe and identify children's movements into sensitive periods when they are best prepared to receive individual lessons in subjects of interest to them that they can grasp readily. Children's senses of autonomy and self-esteem are encouraged in Montessori programs. Montessori instructors also strive to engage parents in their children's education.

What Montessori calls "work" refers to developmentally appropriate learning materials. These are set out so each student can see the choices available. Children can select items from each of Montessori's five sections: Practical Life, Sensorial, Language Arts,

Mathematics and Geometry, and Cultural Subjects. When a child is done with a work, s/he replaces it for another child to use and selects another work. Teachers work one on one with children and in groups; however, the majority of interactions are among children, as Montessori stresses self-directed activity. Not only teachers but also older children help younger ones in learning new skills, so Montessori classes usually incorporate 2- or 3-year age ranges. Depending on students' ages and the individual school, Montessori schooldays are generally half-days, e.g. 9 a.m.–noon or 12:30 p.m. Most Montessori schools also offer afternoon and/or early evening options. Children wanting to "do it myself" benefit from Montessori, as do special-needs children. Individualized attention, independence, and hands-on learning are emphasized. Montessori schools prefer culturally diverse students and teach about diverse cultures.

The Practical Life area of Montessori classes helps children develop care for self, others, and the environment. Children learn many daily skills, including buttoning, pouring liquids, preparing meals, and cleaning up after meals and activities. The Sensorial area gives young children experience with learning through all five senses. They participate in activities like ordering colors from lightest to darkest; sorting objects from roughest to smoothest texture; and sorting items from biggest to smallest/longest to shortest. They learn to match similar tastes, textures, and sounds. The Language Arts area encourages young children to express themselves in words, and they learn to identify letters, match them with corresponding phonemes (speech sounds), and manually trace their shapes as preparation for learning reading, spelling, grammar, and writing. In the Mathematics and Geometry area, children learn to recognize numbers, count, add, subtract, multiply, divide, and use the decimal system via hands-on learning with concrete materials. In the Cultural Subjects area, children learn science, art, music, movement, time, history, geography, and zoology.

Schedules of reinforcement in behaviorism

Continuous schedules of presenting rewards or punishments are fixed. Fixed ratio schedules involve introducing reinforcement after a set number of instances of the targeted behavior. For example, when asking a preschooler to put away materials, a teacher might present punishment for noncompliance only after making three consecutive requests. The disadvantage is, even young children know they can get away with ignoring the first two requests, only complying just before the third. Fixed interval schedules introduce reinforcement after set time periods. Again, the disadvantages are, even multiply disabled infants quickly learn when to expect reinforcement, rather than associating it with how long they have engaged in a desired behavior; young children only change their behavior immediately before the teacher will observe and reward it. Variable ratio and variable interval schedules apply reinforcement following irregular numbers of responses or irregular time periods, respectively. The advantage of variable schedules is, since children cannot predict when they will receive reinforcements, they are more likely to repeat/continue desired behaviors more and for longer times.

Bank Street Curriculum

Lucy Sprague Mitchell founded the Bank Street Curriculum, applying theoretical concepts from Jean Piaget, Erik Erikson, John Dewey, and others. Bank Street is called a Developmental Interaction Approach. It emphasizes children's rich, direct interactions with wide varieties of ideas, materials, and people in their environments. The Bank Street method gives young children opportunities for physical, cognitive, emotional, and social development through engagement in various types of child care programs. Typically, multiple subjects are included and taught to groups. Children can learn through a variety of methods and at different developmental levels. By interacting directly with their geographical, social, and political environments, children are prepared for lifelong learning through this curriculum. Using blocks, solving puzzles, going on field trips, and doing practical lab work are among the numerous learning experiences Bank Street offers. Its philosophy is that school can simultaneously be stimulating, satisfying, and sensible. School is a significant part of children's lives, where they inquire about and experiment with the environment and share ideas with other children as they mature.

The Bank Street Developmental Interaction Approach to teaching recommends that children at the oldest early childhood ages of 5–6 years should have classrooms that are efficient, organized, conducive to working, and designed to afford them sensory and motor learning experiences. Classrooms should include rich varieties of appealing colors, which tend to energize children's imaginations and activity and encourage them to interact with the surroundings and participate in the environment. "Interest corners" in classrooms are advocated by the Bank Street approach. These are places where children can display their art works, use language, and depict social life experiences. This approach also recommends having multipurpose tables in the classroom that children can use for writing, drawing, and other classroom activities. The Bank Street Developmental Interaction Approach also points out the importance of libraries in schools, not just for supporting classroom content, but for providing materials for children's extracurricular reading.

The Bank Street Developmental Interaction Approach requires educators to create well-designed classrooms: this curriculum approach finds children are enabled to develop discipline by growing up in such controlled environments. Teachers are considered to be extremely significant figures in their young students' lives. The Bank Street Approach requires that teachers always treat children with respect, to enable children to develop strong senses of self-respect. Teachers' having faith in their students and believing in their ability to succeed are found to have great impacts on young children's performance and their motivation to excel in school and in life. The Bank Street Curriculum emphasizes the importance of providing transitions from one type of activity to another. It also stresses changing the learning subjects at regular time intervals. This facilitates children's gaining a sense of direction and taking responsibility for what they do. Bank Street views these practices as helping children develop internal self-control, affording them discipline for dealing with the external world.

Froebel's educational theory

Friedrich Froebel (1782–1852) invented the original concept and practice of Kindergarten. His theory of education had widespread influences, including using play-based instruction with young children. Froebel's educational theory emphasized the unity of humanity, nature, and God. Froebel believed the success of the individual dictates the success of the race, and that school's role is to direct students' will. He believed nature is the heart of all learning. He felt unity, individuality, and diversity were important values achieved through education. Froebel said education's goals include developing self-control and spirituality. He recommended curricula include math, language, design, art, health, hygiene, and physical education. He noted school's role in social development. According to Froebel, schools should impart meaning to life experiences; show students relationships among external, previously unrelated knowledge; and associate facts with principles. Froebel felt human potential is defined through individual accomplishments. He believed humans generally are productive and creative, attaining completeness and harmony via maturation.

Froebel, 19th-century inventor of Kindergarten, developed an influential educational theory. He found that observation, discovery, play, and free, self-directed activity facilitated children's learning. He observed that drawing/art activities develop higher level cognitive skills and that virtues are taught through children's games. He also found nature, songs, fables, stories, poems, and crafts effective learning media. He attributed reading and writing development to children's self-expression needs. Froebel recommended activities to develop children's motor skills and stimulate their imaginations. He believed in equal rather than authoritarian teacher-student relationships, and advocated family involvement/collaboration. He pointed out the critical nature of sensory experiences, and the value of life experiences for self-expression. He believed teachers should support students' discovery learning rather than prescribing what to learn. Like Piaget, Dewey, and Montessori, Froebel embraced constructivist learning, i.e. children construct meaning and reality through their interactions with the environment. He stressed the role of parents, particularly mothers, in children's educational processes.

Friedrich Froebel originated the concept and practice of Kindergarten (German for "child's garden") in 1837. His educational theory had great influence on early childhood education. Froebel's theory addressed society's role in education. He saw education as defined by the "law of divine unity," which stated that everything is connected and humanity, nature, and God are unified. Froebel believed all developments are by God's plan; he found the social institution of religion an important part of children's education. He emphasized parental and sibling involvement in child education. He theorized that culture is changed not by acquiring ideas, but by the productivity, work, and actions of the individual. Froebel believed all children deserve respect and individual attention; should develop their individual potentials; and can learn, irrespective of social class or religion, providing they are developmentally ready for given specific content. Regarding consensus, Froebel's view was religious: he believed God's supreme plan determined social and moral order. He felt people should share common experiences and learn unity, while also respecting diversity and individuality.

Siegfried Engelmann

Engelmann (b. 1931) cofounded the Bereiter-Engelmann Program with Carl Bereiter with funding from the U.S. Office of Education. This project demonstrated the ability of intensive instruction to enhance cognitive skills in disadvantaged preschool-aged children, establishing the Bereiter-Engelmann Preschool Program. Bereiter and Engelmann also conducted experiments reexamining Piaget's theory of cognitive development, specifically concerning the ability to conserve liquid volume. They showed, contrary to Piaget's contention that this ability depended solely on a child's cognitive-developmental stage, it could be taught. Engelmann researched curriculum and instruction, including preschoolers with Down syndrome and children from impoverished backgrounds, establishing the philosophy and methodology of Direct Instruction. He designed numerous reading, math, spelling, language, and writing instruction programs, and also achievement tests, videos, and games. Engelmann worked with Project Head Start and Project Follow Through. The former included his and Wesley Becker's comparison of their Engelmann-Becker model of early childhood instruction with other models in teaching disadvantaged children. The latter is often considered the biggest controlled study ever comparing teaching models and methods.

In the 1960s, Siegfried Engelmann noted a lack of research into how young children learn. Wanting to find out what kinds of teaching effected retention, and what the extent was of individual differences among young learners, Engelmann conducted research, as Piaget had done, using his own children and those of colleagues and neighbors. With a previous advertising background, Engelmann formed focus groups of preschool children to test-market teaching methods. Main features of the curricula Engelmann developed included emphasizing phonics and computation early in young children's instruction; using a precise logical sequence to teach new skills; teaching new skills in small, separate, "child-sized" pieces; correcting learners' errors immediately; adhering strictly to designated teaching schedules; constantly reviewing to integrate new learning with previously attained knowledge; and scrupulous measurement techniques for assessing skills mastery. To demonstrate the results of his methods for teaching math, Engelmann sent movies he made of these to educational institutions. They showed that with his methods, toddlers could master upper-elementary-grade-level computations, and even simple linear equations.

Direct Instruction method

Direct Instruction (DI) is a behavioral method of teaching. Therefore, learner errors receive immediate corrective feedback, and correct responses receive immediate, obvious positive reinforcement. DI has a fast pace—10–14 learner responses per minute overall—affording more attention and less boredom; reciprocal teacher-student feedback; immediate indications of learner problems to teachers; and natural reinforcement of teacher activities. DI thus promotes more mutual student and teacher learning than traditional "one-way" methods. Children are instructed in small groups according to ability levels. Their attention is teacher-focused. Teacher presentations follow scripts designed to give instruction the proper sequence, including prewritten prompts and questions developed through field-testing with real students. These optimized prepared lessons allow teachers to attend to extra instructional and motivational aspects of learning. Cued by teachers, who control the pace and give all learners with varying response rates chances for practice, children respond actively in groups and individually. Small groups are typically seated in semicircles close to teachers, who use visual aids like blackboards and overhead projectors.

Project Follow Through

In 1967, President Lyndon B. Johnson declared his War on Poverty. This initiative included Project Follow Through, funded by the U.S. Office of Education and Office of Economic Opportunity. Research had previously found that Project Head Start, which offered early educational interventions to disadvantaged preschoolers, had definite positive impacts; but these were often short-lived. Project Follow Through was intended to discover how to maintain Head Start's benefits. Siegfried Engelmann and Wesley Becker, who had developed the Engelmann-Becker instructional model, invited others to propose various other teaching models in communities selected to participate in Project Follow Through. The researchers asked parents in each community to choose from among the models provided. The proponents of each model were given funds to train teachers and furnish curriculum. Models found to enhance disadvantaged children's school achievement were to be promoted nationally. Engelmann's Direct Instruction model showed positive results surpassing all other models. However, the U.S. Office of Education did not adopt this or other models found best.

A huge comparative study of curriculum and instruction methods, Project Follow Through incorporated three main approaches: Affective, Basic Skills, and Cognitive. Affective approaches used in Project Follow Through included the Bank Street, Responsive Education, and Open Education models. These teaching models aim to enhance school achievement by emphasizing experiences that raise children's self-esteem, which is believed to facilitate their acquisition of basic skills and higher-order problem-solving skills. Basic Skills approaches included the Southwest Labs, Behavior Analysis, and Direct Instruction models. These models find that mastering basic skills facilitates higher-order cognitive and problem-solving skills, and higher self-esteem. Cognitive approaches included the Parent Education, TEEM, and Cognitively Oriented Curriculum models. These models focus on teaching higher-order problem-solving and thinking skills as the optimal avenue to enhancing school achievement, and to improving lower-order basic skills and self-esteem. Affective and Cognitive models have become popular in most schools of education. Basic Skills approaches are less popular, but are congruent with other, very effective methods of specialized instruction.

Constance Kamii

Professor of early childhood education Constance Kamii, of Japanese ancestry, was born in Geneva, Switzerland. She attended elementary school in both Switzerland and Japan, completing secondary school and higher education degrees in the United States. She studied extensively with Jean Piaget, also of Geneva. She worked with the Perry Preschool Project in the 1960s, fueling her subsequent interest in theoretically grounded instruction. Kamii believes in basing early childhood educational goals and objectives upon scientific theory of children's cognitive, social, and moral development; and moreover that Piaget's theory of cognitive development is the sole explanation for child development from birth to adolescence. She has done much curriculum research in the U.S., and published a number of books, on how to apply Piaget's theory practically in early childhood classrooms. Kamii agrees with Piaget that education's overall, long-term goal is developing children's intellectual, social, and moral autonomy. Kamii has said, "A classroom cannot foster the development of autonomy in the intellectual realm while suppressing it in the social and moral realms."

Kamii-DeVries

Constance Kamii and Rhetta DeVries formulated the Kamii-DeVries Constructivist Perspective model of preschool education. It is closely based upon Piaget's theory of child cognitive development and on the Constructivist theory to which Piaget and others subscribed, which dictates that children construct their own realities through their interactions with the environment. Piaget's particular constructivism included the principle that through their interacting with the world within a logical-mathematical structure, children's intelligence, knowledge, personalities, and morality develop. The Kamii-DeVries approach finds that children learn via performing mental actions, which Piaget called operations, through the vehicle of physical activities. This model favors using teachers experienced in traditional preschool education, who employ a child-centered approach, and establish active learning settings, are in touch with children's thoughts, respond to children from children's perspectives, and facilitate children's extension of their ideas. The Kamii-

- 74 -

DeVries model has recently been applied to learning assessments using technology (2003) and to using constructivism in teaching physics to preschoolers (2011).

High/Scope Curriculum

The High/Scope Curriculum, developed by David P. Weikart and colleagues, takes a constructivist approach influenced by Piaget's theory, advocating active learning. The High/Scope curriculum model identified a total of 58 "key experiences" it finds critical for preschool child development and learning. These key experiences are subdivided into ten main categories: (1) Creative representation, which includes recognizing symbolic use, imitating, and playing roles; (2) Language and literacy, which include speaking, describing, scribbling, and narrating/dictating stories; (3) Initiative and social relations, including solving problems, making decisions and choices, and building relationships; (4) Movement, including activities like running, bending, stretching, and dancing; (5) Music, which includes singing, listening to music, and playing musical instruments; (6) Classification, which includes sorting objects, matching objects or pictures, and describing object shapes; (7) Seriation, or arranging things in prescribed orders (e.g. by size or number); (8) Numbers, which for preschoolers focuses on counting; (9) Space, which involves activities like filling and emptying containers; and (10) Time, including concepts of starting, sequencing, and stopping actions.

David Weikart and colleagues developed the High/Scope Curriculum in the 1960s and 1970s, testing it in the Perry Preschool and Head Start Projects, among others. The High/Scope philosophy is based on Piaget's Constructivist principles that active learning is optimal for young children; that they need to become involved actively with materials, ideas, people, and events; and that children and teachers learn together in the instructional environment. Weikart and colleagues' early research focused on economically disadvantaged children, but the High/Scope approach has since been extended to all young children and all kinds of preschool settings. This model recommends dividing classrooms into well-furnished, separate "interest areas," and regular daily class routines affording children time to plan, implement, and reflect upon what they learn, and to participate in large and small group activities. Teachers establish socially supportive atmospheres; plan group learning activities; organize settings and set daily routines; encourage purposeful child activities, problem-solving, and verbal reflection; and interpret child behaviors according to High/Scope's key child development experiences.

The High/Scope Curriculum frequently incorporates computers as regular program components, including developmentally appropriate software, for children to access when they choose. School days may be full-day or part-day, determined by each individual program. Flexible hours accommodate individual family needs and situations. High/Scope programs work in both child care and preschool settings. High/Scope was originally designed to enhance educational outcomes for young children considered at-risk due to socioeconomically disadvantaged, urban backgrounds, and was compatible with Project Head Start. This model of early childhood curriculum and instruction advocates individualizing teaching to each child's developmental level and pace of learning. As such, the High/Scope approach is found to be effective for children who have learning disabilities, and also for children with developmental delays. It works well with all children needing individual attention. High/Scope is less amenable to highly structured settings that use more adult-directed instruction.

Head Start Program

Head Start was begun in 1964, extended by the Head Start Act of 1981, and revised in its 2007 reauthorization. It is a program of the U.S. Department of Health and Human Services designed to give low-income families and their young children comprehensive services of health, nutrition, education, and parental involvement. While Head Start was initially intended to "catch up" low-income children over the summer to reach kindergarten readiness, it soon became obvious that a six-week preschool program was inadequate to compensate for having lived in poverty for one's first five years. Hence the Head Start Program was expanded and modified over the years with the aim of remediating the effects of system-wide poverty upon child educational outcomes. Currently, Head Start gives local public, private, nonprofit, and for-profit agencies grants for delivering comprehensive child development services to promote disadvantaged children's school readiness by improving their cognitive and social development. It particularly emphasizes developing early reading and math abilities preschoolers will need for school success.

The Early Head Start program developed as an outgrowth of the original Head Start Program. Head Start initially aimed to remediate the deprivation of poor preschool-aged children by providing educational services over the summer to help them attain school readiness by kindergarten. Because educators and researchers soon discovered the summer program was insufficient to make up for poor children's lack of preparation, Head Start was expanded to become more comprehensive. Head Start was established in 1964 and expanded by the Head Start Act in 1981. After research had accumulated considerable evidence of how important children's earliest years are to their ensuing growth and development, the U.S. Department of Health and Human Services Administration for Children and Families' Office of Head Start established the Early Head Start Program in 1995. Early Head Start works to improve prenatal health; improve infant and toddler development; and enhance healthy family functioning. It serves children from 0–3 years. Like the original program, Early Head Start stresses parental engagement in children's growth, development, and learning.

Emergent literacy theory

(1) According to the theory of emergent literacy, even infants encounter written language. Two- and three-year-olds commonly can identify logos, labels, and signs in their homes and communities. Also, young children's scribbles show features/appearances of their language's specific writing system even before they can write. For example, Egyptian children's scribbles look more like Egyptian writing; American children's scribbles look more like English writing. (2) Young children learn to read and write concurrently, not sequentially; the two abilities are closely interrelated. Moreover, though with speech, receptive language comprehension seems easier/sooner to develop than expressive language production, this does not apply to reading and writing: first learning activities involving writing are found easier for preschoolers than those involving reading. (3) Research finds that form follows function, not the opposite: young children's literacy learning is mostly through meaningful, functional, purposeful/goal-directed real-life activities. Literacy comprises not isolated, abstract skills learned for their own sake, but rather authentic skills applied to accomplish real-life purposes, the way children observe adults using literacy.

Through extensive research, emergent literacy theorists have found that: (1) Young children develop literacy through being actively involved in reading and rereading their favorite storybooks. When preschoolers "reread" storybooks, they have not memorized them; rather, theorists find this activity to exemplify young children's reconstruction of a book's meaning. Similarly, young children's invented spellings are examples of their efforts to reconstruct what they know of written language; they can inform us about a child's familiarity with specific phonetic components. (2) Adults' reading to children, no matter how young, is crucial to literacy development. It helps children gain a "feel" for the character, flow, and patterns of written/printed language, and an overall sense of what reading feels like and entails. It fosters positive attitudes toward reading in children, strongly motivating them to read when they begin school. Being read to also helps children develop print awareness and formulate concepts of books and reading. (3) Influenced by Piaget and Vygotsky, emergent literacy theory views reading and writing as developmental processes having successive stages.

Emergent literacy vs. reading readiness

Historically, early childhood educators viewed "reading readiness" as a time during young children's literacy development when they were ready to start learning to read and write, and taught literacy accordingly. However, in the late 20th and early 20th centuries, research has found that children have innate learning capacities and that skills emerge under the proper conditions. Educational researchers came to view language as developing gradually within a child rather than a child's being ready to read at a certain time. Thus, the term "emergent" came to replace "readiness," while "literacy" replaced "reading" as referring to all of language's interrelated aspects of listening, speaking, writing, and viewing, as well as reading. Traditional views of literacy were based only on children's reading and writing in ways similar to those of adults. However, more recently, the theory of emergent literacy has evolved through the findings of research into the early preschool reading of young children and their and their families' associated characteristics.

The emergent literacy theoretical perspective yields an instructional model for the learning and teaching of reading and writing in young children that is founded on building instruction from the child's knowledge. Emergent literacy theory's assumption is that young children already know a lot about language and literacy by the time they enter school. This theory furthermore regards even 2- and 3-year-olds as having information about how the reading and writing processes function, and as having already formed particular ideas about what written/printed language is. From this perspective, emergent literacy theory then dictates that teaching should build upon what a child already knows and should support the child's further literacy development. Researchers conclude that teachers should furnish open-ended activities allowing children to show what they already know about literacy; to apply that knowledge; and to build upon it. From the emergent literacy perspective, teachers take the role of creating a learning environment with conditions that are conducive to children's learning in ways that are ideally self-motivated, self-generated, and self-regulated.

Literacy practices that are not developmentally appropriate

Research finds some preschools are like play centers, but not optimal for literacy because their curricula exclude natural reading and writing activities. Researchers have also identified a trend in many kindergartens to ensure children's "reading readiness" by providing highly academic programs, influencing preschool curricula to get children "ready" for such kindergartens. Influenced and even pressured by kindergarten programs' academic expectations, parents have also come to expect preschools to prepare their children for kindergarten. However, experts find applying elementary-school programs to kindergartens and preschools developmentally inappropriate. Formal instruction in reading and writing and worksheets are not suitable for younger children. Instead, research finds print-rich preschool environments both developmentally appropriate and more effective. For example, when researchers changed classrooms from having a "book corner" to having a centrally located table with books plus paper, pencils, envelopes, and stamps, children spent 3 to 10 times more time on direct reading and writing activities. Children are found to take naturally to these activities without prior formal reading and writing lessons.

Planning a play-based curriculum

To plan a curriculum based on children's natural play with building blocks (Hoisington, 2008), a teacher can first arrange the environment to stimulate further such play. Then s/he can furnish materials for children to make plans/blueprints for and records and models of buildings they construct. The teacher can make time during the day for children to reflect upon and discuss their individual and group building efforts. Teachers can also utilize teaching strategies that encourage children to reflect on and consider in more depth the scientific principles related to their results. A teacher can provide building materials of varied sizes, shapes, textures, and weights, and props to add realism, triggering more complex structures and creative, dramatic, emotional, and social development. Teachers can take photos of children's structures as documents for discussions, stimulating language and vocabulary development. Supplying additional materials to support and stick together blocks extends play-based learning. Active teacher participation by offering observations and asking open-ended questions promotes children's standards-based learning of scientific, mathematical, and linguistic concepts, processes, and patterns.

When children play at building with blocks, for example, they investigate material properties such as various block shapes, sizes, and weights and the stability of carpet vs. hard floor as bases. They explore cause-and-effect relationships; make conclusions regarding the results of their trial-and-error experiments; draw generalizations about observed patterns; and form theories about what does and does not work to build high towers. Ultimately, they construct their knowledge of how reality functions. Teachers support this by introducing relevant learning standards in the play context meaningful to children. For example, math standards including spatial awareness, geometry, number, operations, patterns, and measurement can be supported through planning play. By encouraging and guiding children's discussion and documentation of their play constructions, and supplying nonfictional and fictional books about building, a teacher also integrates learning goals and objectives for language and literacy development. Teachers can plan activities specifically to extend learning in these domains, like counting blocks; comparison/contrast; matching; sorting; sequencing; phonological awareness; alphabetic awareness; print awareness; book appreciation; listening, comprehension, speech, and communication.

Thematic teaching units

To develop a thematic teaching unit, a teacher designs a collection of related activities around certain themes or topics that crosses several curriculum areas or domains. Thematic units create learning environments for young children that promote all children's active engagement, as well as their process learning. By studying topics children find relevant to their own lives, thematic units build upon children's preexisting knowledge and current interests, and also help them relate information to their own life experiences. Varied curriculum content can be more easily integrated through thematic units, in ways that young children can understand and apply meaningfully. Children's diverse individual learning styles are also accommodated through thematic units. Such units involve children physically in learning; teach them factual information in greater depth; teach them learning process-related skills, i.e. "learning how to learn"; holistically integrate learning; encourage cohesion in groups; meet children's individual needs; and provide motivation to both children and their teachers.

Project Approach

The Project Approach (Katz and Chard, 1989) entails having young children choose a topic interesting to them, studying this topic, researching it, and solving problems and questions as they emerge. This gives children greater practice with creative thinking and problem-solving skills, which supports greater success in all academic and social areas. For example, if a class of preschoolers shows interest in the field of medicine, their teacher can plan a field trip to a local hospital to introduce a project studying medicine in depth. During the trip, the teacher can write down/record children's considerations and questions, and then use these as guidelines to plan and conduct relevant activities that will further stimulate the children's curiosity and imagination. Throughout this or any other in-depth project, the teacher can integrate specific skills for reading, writing, math, science, social studies, and creative thinking. This affords dual benefits: enabling both children's skills advancement, and their gaining knowledge they recognize is required and applies in their own lives. Children become life-long learners with this recognition.

Integrated curriculum

An integrated curriculum organizes early childhood education to transcend the boundaries between the various domains and subject content areas. It unites different curriculum elements through meaningful connections to allow study of wider areas of knowledge. It treats learning holistically and mirrors the interactive nature of reality. The principle that learning consists of series of interconnections is the foundation for teaching through use of an integrated curriculum. Benefits of integrated curricula include an organized planning mechanism; greater flexibility; and the ability to teach many skills and concepts effectively, include more varied content, and enable children to learn most naturally. By identifying themes children find most interesting, teachers can construct webs of assorted themes, which can provide the majority of their curriculum. Research has proven the effectiveness of integrated teaching units for both children and their teachers. Teachers can also integrate new content into existing teaching units they have identified as effective. Integrated units enable teachers to ensure children are learning pertinent knowledge and applying it to real-life situations.

EC teachers can incorporate many skills into units organized by theme. This includes state governments' educational standards/benchmarks for various skills. Teachers can base units on topics of interest to young children, e.g. building construction, space travel, movie-making, dinosaurs, vacations, nursery rhymes, fairy tales, pets, wildlife, camping, the ocean, and studies of particular authors and book themes. Beginning with a topic that motivates the children is best; related activities and skills will naturally follow. In planning units, teachers should establish connections among content areas like literacy, physical activity, dramatic play, art, music, math, science, and social studies. Making these connections permits children's learning through their strongest/favored modalities and supports learning through meaningful experiences, which is how they learn best. Theme-based approaches effectively address individual differences and modality-related strengths, as represented in Gardner's theory of Multiple Intelligences. Thematic approaches facilitate creating motivational learning centers and hands-on learning activities, and are also compatible with creating portfolio assessments and performance-based assessments. Teachers can encompass skill and conceptual benchmarks for specific age/developmental levels within engaging themes.

Integrating subject/domain content across the curriculum has been used for years at every educational level, from higher education to early childhood education. However, recent demands for accountability, as exemplified and escalated by No Child Left Behind, can distract educators from holistic and overall learning toward preoccupation with developing isolated skills and using test scores to measure achievement. But rather than discarding teaching methods proven effective, early childhood educators need to integrate newer, mandate-related practices into existing plans and methods. Teaching integrated curricula in early childhood classrooms has proven effective for both children and teachers. Integrating learning domains and subject content in turn integrates the child's developing skills with the whole child. When teachers use topics children find interesting and exciting, in-depth projects focusing on particular themes, and good children's literature, they give children motivation to learn the important concepts and skills they need for school and life success. Children should bring home from preschool not only further developed skills, but also knowledge useful and meaningful in life.

Teaching and Learning

Whole language approach to teaching child literacy

The whole language approach is based on constructivist philosophy and psychology: children construct their own knowledge through their interactions with their environments. In contrast to analytical approaches like phonics and alphabetic learning, constructivism views learning as an individual's unique cognitive experience of acquiring new knowledge, shaped by the individual's existing knowledge and personal perspective. Whole language instruction emphasizes helping children create meaning from their reading and express meaning in their writing. The whole-language philosophy emphasizes cultural diversity, integrating literacy instruction across subject domains, reading high-quality literature, and giving children many opportunities for independent reading, small-group guided reading, and being read to aloud by teachers. Whole language believes children learn to read by writing and vice versa. Realistically purposeful reading and writing are encouraged, as is using texts that motivate children to develop a love for literature. Early grammatical/spelling/technical correctness is not stressed, which can be problematic for children with reading/language processing disorders, who need explicit instruction in decoding skills and strategies.

The whole language approach concentrates on children's seeking, finding, and constructing meaning in language. As such, young children's early technical correctness is not the priority. Whole language teachers do not ignore children's errors. However, they do not make correction more important than overall engagement, understanding, and appreciation of reading, writing, and literature. Instead, teachers make formative assessments taking into account the errors each child makes. Then they design learning experiences for children that give them opportunities and assistance in acquiring mechanically correct linguistic forms and structures. While this holistic approach finds analytical techniques that break language down into components like phonemes and alphabet letters less useful, children with language processing/reading problems need to learn phonemic awareness, phonics, and other decoding skills to develop reading fluency. The National Reading Panel conducted a study (1997–2000) to resolve controversy over phonics vs. whole language as the best teaching method, finding that any effective reading instruction program must teach phonemic awareness, phonics, reading fluency, vocabulary development, and reading comprehension.

Language Experience Approach (LEA)

The LEA teaches beginning reading by connecting students' personal life experiences with written/printed words. A unique benefit is students using their own language and words, enabling them to interact with texts on multiple levels simultaneously. They thus realize they acquire knowledge and understanding through not just instruction, but also their own experiences. Four steps for implementing the LEA with EC groups: (1) Children and teacher choose a topic, like an exciting trip, game, or recent TV show, to discuss with teacher guidance. (2) Each child takes a turn saying a sentence using his/her own words that advances the discussion/story. The teacher writes the children's words verbatim without corrections, visibly and clearly. (3) Every few sentences or several words, the teacher stops and reads the record aloud for children to confirm accuracy. (4) Record review: the teacher points to each word, they read aloud together, or children repeat after the teacher. The teacher gives children copies of the record for independent review and possible compilation into books of LEA stories.

Basal reader approach

The basal reader is America's commonest approach, used in an estimated 75–85 percent of K–8th-grade classrooms. The number of publishers offering basal reading series has decreased to about one-fourth of that in the 20th century, decreasing teacher responsibility for investigating/piloting readers for district approval. Using basal readers is a skills-based/bottom-up approach. Teaching smaller-to-larger reading subskills in systematic, rigid sequence assists students' transition from part to whole. Texts graded by reading level contain narration and exposition organized thematically by unit, including children's literature and diverse other genres. Phonics and other specific instructional strands with practice assignments develop skills, which are assessed with end-of-unit tests. For young children, text decoding is enabled through exact control of vocabulary items and word analysis skills, "big [enlarged] books," and word and picture cards. 20th-century and older series sacrificed comprehension and enjoyment for vocabulary control and skill acquisition, but 21st-century series vary methods more (like multiple story versions or book excerpts enabling selection sharing), affording children more motivation to read.

Directed reading activity

Using basal readers, the DRA comprises: (1) The teacher prepares children for reading by stimulating their motivation and introducing new concepts and/or vocabulary. (2) Students read silently, guided by teacher questions and statements. (3) The teacher develops student comprehension and students discuss characters, plots, or concepts to further comprehension. (4) After silent reading, students read aloud and read answers to teacher questions, known as "purposeful rereading." (5) Students' follow-up workbook activities/practice review comprehension and vocabulary. Some selections may include enrichment activities relating them to writing, art, drama, or music. The DR-TA approach is designed to develop critical readers through instruction in group comprehension. It requires children's active engagement in reading by processing information, asking questions, and receiving feedback as they read. The first phase of DR-TA is the teacher's direction of student thought processes throughout reading. The second phase involves developing student skills according to their needs as identified in phase 1, and additional extension or follow-up activities.

Directed reading activity (DRA) vs. directed reading-thinking activity (DR-TA)

(1) One main difference is that the DR-TA approach gives teachers all the responsibility and greater flexibility for developing lessons. As such it contains fewer directions than the DRA approach, which contains specific materials and questions to use, specific guidelines, and is more teacher-manual-oriented and materials-oriented. Therefore DR-TA can be used for not only basal readers, but also planning lessons in other curriculum areas involving reading; the DRA approach applies more directly to basal reader programs. (2) DRA manuals use mostly literal, factual questions, requiring only convergent thinking for student responses. However, in DR-TA, questions also demand divergent (creative) thinking of students, stimulating higher-level reading comprehension and interpretation. (3) New vocabulary is pretaught in the DRA approach before children read. The DR-TA approach excludes preteaching, realistically requiring student decoding of new vocabulary words

- 82 -

during reading. (4) DRA manuals specify when to teach which skills for reading comprehension. DR-TA approaches do not, requiring more questioning expertise and acceptance of some alternative student responses by teachers.

Manipulatives used for preschool math learning

Young children learn primarily through visually inspecting, touching, holding, and manipulating concrete objects. While they are less likely to understand abstract concepts presented abstractly, such concepts are likelier accessible to preschoolers through the medium of real things they can see, feel, and manipulate. Manipulatives are proven as effective learning devices; some early math curricula (e.g. Horizons) even require them. They are also particularly useful for children with tactile or visual learning styles. Many math manipulatives are available for sale, e.g. linking cubes; 3-dimensional geometric shapes and "geoboards"; large magnetized numbers for whiteboards; weights, scales, and balances for measurements; math blocks; math games; number boards and color tiles; flash cards; play money, toy cash registers, and activities; objects for sorting and patterning; or tangrams for recognizing shapes, reproducing and designing patterns, and spatial problem-solving. Teachers can create homemade math manipulatives using bottle caps/lids; seashells, pebbles/stones; buttons; keys; variously sized, shaped, and colored balls; coffee stirrers; or cardboard tubes from paper products.

Process skills that preschool science programs help develop

Experts find three process skills that good EC science programs help develop are observation, classification, and communication. Young children are inherently curious about the world and hence enjoy many activities involving inquiry and discovery. Teachers can uncover science in many existing preschool activities. For example, since young children relate to activities focusing on themselves, teachers can have them construct skeletons of dry pasta, using their pictures as heads. Cooking activities involve science, as do art activities. Teachers can have children explore various substances' solubility in water, which colors are produced by mixing which other colors, etc. They can have them compare/contrast similarities/differences among objects. They can create inexpensive science centers using animal puppets; models; thematically-related games, puzzles, books, and writing materials; mirrors, prisms, magnifiers; scales, magnets; and various observable, measurable objects. Teachers should regularly vary materials to sustain children's interest.

Using inquiry and discovery in science

EC teachers are advised to "teach what they know," i.e. use materials with which they are familiar. For example, teachers who like plants can have young children plant beans, water and watch them grow, moreover incorporating this activity with the story "Jack and the Beanstalk." Teachers can bring in plants, leaves, and flowers for children to observe and measure their sizes, shapes, or textures. Experts recommend teachers utilize their everyday environments to procure learning materials, such as pine needles and cones; loose feathers and leaves found outdoors; animal fur from pets or groomers; and/or snakeskins or turtle shells from local pet stores. Experts advise teachers to use their observational skills during inquiry and discovery activities: if children apply nonstandard and/or unusual uses of some materials, teachers should observe what could be a new discovery, wherein students teach adults new learning, too. Teachers should let children play with and explore new materials to understand their purposes, uses, and care before using them in structured activities.

Developing physical coordination, fine motor skills, and large muscle skills

Preschoolers are more likely to fall because their lower bodies are not yet developed equally to their upper bodies, giving them higher centers of gravity. Therefore, seeing how long they can balance on one foot and hopping exercises help improve balance and coordination. Hopping races let preschoolers participate in groups and observe peer outcomes, which can also enhance self-confidence and supporting others. "Freeze dancing" (like Musical Chairs without the chair-sitting), without eliminations, provides physical activity and improves coordination. Using writing implements, tying shoes, and playing with small items develop fine motor skills. With preschoolers, it is more effective and developmentally appropriate to incorporate fine motor activities into playtime than to separate quiet activity from play. For example, on nature walks, teachers can have children collect pebbles and twigs and throw them into a stream, developing coordination and various muscles. Running, skipping, and playing tag develop large muscle skills. Kicking, throwing, and catching balls give good unstructured exercise without game rules preschoolers cannot understand. Preschoolers' short attention spans preclude long activity durations.

Aesthetic experiences

Aesthetic experiences focusing on color

To help children learn color names and develop sensory discrimination and classification abilities, some art museums offer preschool lessons, which teachers can also use as models. For example, a teacher can read a children's story or sing a song about color, then present a painting/artwork for children to examine, and then a separate display with circles/squares/ovals of colors used by the artist, asking children to name these and any other colors they know, and identify any other colors the artist used not represented in the second display. The teacher then demonstrates how mixing produces other colors. After this demonstration with children's discussion, the teacher gives each child a piece of heavy-duty paper and a brush. The teacher pours about an inch-sized puddle of each of the three primary colors—red, blue, and yellow—in the middle of each child's paper. The teacher then tells the children to use their brushes to explore mixing colors and see the variety of other colors they can create.

Aesthetic experiences involving shape

Giving young children learning activities that focus on shape used in art helps them develop their abilities to form concepts and identify discrepancies. Manipulating basic geometric shapes also stimulates their creative thinking skills and imaginations, as well as developing early geometric math skills. For example, an EC teacher can first read aloud a children's book about shapes, of which many are available. After reading it through, the teacher can go back through the story asking children to point to and name shapes they recognize. Then the teacher can show children an artwork. Using line drawings and/or solid geometric shapes, they discuss what shapes the artist used. The teacher can help children arrange solid shapes to form different images (people, flowers, houses). The teacher can then give children paper pulp trays/heavy paper/board, assorted wooden/cardboard/plastic shapes, and instructions to think and arrange shapes they can make with them, and then give them glue to affix the shapes to their trays/paper/board. They can paint their creations after the glue dries.

Element of line in visual art

Activities focusing on line in art help young children expand their symbol recognition, develop their comparison-making ability, and facilitate shape recognition. Teachers can begin by singing a song or reading a children's story about lines. Then they can present one painting/drawing/artwork and help children point at various kinds of lines that the artist used. The teacher can draw various line types on a separate piece of paper, e.g. wavy, pointy, spiral, and ask children to find similar lines in the artwork. Then the teacher can ask children to try drawing these different lines themselves. Teachers should also inform children of various tools for drawing lines and let them experiment with these, e.g. crayons, pencils, markers, chalk, paint. An EC teacher can also supply butcher paper or other roll paper for each child to lie down on in whatever creative body positions they can make. The teacher outlines their body shapes with a marker. Then the teacher has the children explore drawing different kinds of lines, using various kinds of drawing tools, to enhance and personalize their individual body outlines.

Element of texture in art

Preschoolers learn much through looking at and touching concrete materials. Activities involving visual and tactile examination and manipulation plus verbal discussion enhance young children's representational/symbolic thinking abilities. Such activities also enable children to explore various ways of representing different textures visually. Teachers can provide "feely bags/boxes"—bags/boxes with variously textured items inside, e.g. sandpaper, fleece, clay, wool, or tree bark—for children to feel and describe textures before seeing them, and identify objects based on feel. A teacher can then show children a selected artwork; they discuss together which textures are included, e.g. smooth, rough, jagged, bumpy, sharp, prickly, soft, or slippery. The teacher can then demonstrate using plaster/thickened paste/clay how to create various textures using assorted tools (e.g. tongue depressors, plastic tableware, chopsticks, small toys, or child-safe pottery tools) and have children experiment with discovering and producing as many different textures as they can. After children's products dry, they can paint them the next day.

Social skills

Experts find it crucial for young children's later success in school and life to have experiences that develop understanding of their own and others' emotions; constructive management of their strong feelings; and skills in forming and maintaining relationships. Young children use earlier developed motor skills like pushing/shoving, biting, hitting, or kicking, to get what they want rather than later developing verbal skills. Since physical aggression is antisocial, social development includes learning more acceptable, verbal emotional expressions. "Punch and Judy"–type puppet-shows depicting aggression's failures entertain preschoolers; discussing puppet behavior develops social skills. Teachers have children say which puppets they liked/disliked and considered good/bad; what happened; what might happen next; and how puppets could act differently. Teachers can reinforce children's discussion of meeting needs using words, not violence. Many read-aloud stories explain why people behave certain ways in social contexts; discussion/question-and-answer groups promote empathy, understanding, and listening skills. Assigning collaborative projects, like scrapbooking in small groups, helps young children learn cooperation, turn taking, listening, and verbally expressing what they want.

Affective learning experiences

Providing affective experiences supports young children's emotional development, including understanding and expressing their emotions. These enable development of emotional self-regulation/self-control. Emotional development is also prerequisite to and supportive of social interactions and development. Affective activities also help teachers understand how children feel, which activities they find most fascinating, and/or why they are not participating. "Feelings and Faces" activities are useful. For example, a teacher can have each child draw four different "feeling" faces on paper plates—e.g. happy, sad, angry, confused, excited—and discuss each. A teacher can offer various scenarios, like learning a new song, painting a picture, getting a new pet, or feeling sick, and ask children how they feel about each. Then the teacher can give them new paper plates, having them draw faces showing feelings they often have. Gluing Popsicle sticks to the plates turns them into "masks." The teacher can prompt the children on later days to hold up their masks to illustrate how they feel on a given day and about specific activities/experiences.

<u>Providing affective experiences and promoting emotional development, physical activity, and creativity</u>
Early childhood teachers can help children understand their feelings and others' feelings, express their emotions, engage in physical exercise, use creative thinking, and have fun by using emotional movement activities. For example, the teacher can begin with prompting the children to demonstrate various types of body movements and postures, like crawling, walking, tiptoeing, skipping, hopping, crouching, slouching, limping, or dancing. Then the teacher can ask the children which feelings they associate with each type of movement and body position. The teacher can play some music for children to move to, and give them instructions such as "Move like you are happy....like you are sad....like you are scared....like you are surprised....like you are angry...." Teachers can also use "freeze"/"statue" dances or games, wherein children move to music and must freeze in position like statues when the music stops; for affective practice, teachers instruct children to depict a certain emotion each time they freeze in place.

Indoor and outdoor space

Indoor and outdoor EC learning environments should be safe, clean, and attractive. They should include at least 35' square indoors and 75' square outdoors of usable play space per child. Staff must have access to prepare spaces before children's arrival. Gyms/other larger indoor spaces can substitute if outdoor spaces are smaller. The youngest children should be given separate outdoor times/places. Outdoor scheduling should ensure enough room, plus prevent altercations/competition among different age groups. Teachers can assess if enough space exists by observing children's interactions and engagement in activities. Children's products and other visuals should be displayed at child's-eye level. Spaces should be arranged to allow individual, small-group, and large-group activity. Space organization should create clear pathways enabling children to move easily among activities without overly disturbing others, should promote positive social interactions and behaviors; and activities in each area should not distract children in other areas.

Learning environments

Arranging indoor learning environments according to curricular activities
EC experts indicate that rooms should be organized to enable various activities, but not necessarily to limit activities to certain areas. For example, mathematical and scientific preschool activities may occur in multiple parts of a classroom, though the room should still be laid out to facilitate their occurrence. Sufficient space for infants to crawl and toddlers to toddle are necessary, as are both hard and carpeted floors. Bolted-down/heavy, sturdy furniture is needed for infants and toddlers to use for pulling up, balancing, and cruising. Art and cooking activities should be positioned near sinks/water sources for cleanup. Designating separate areas for activities like block-building, book-reading, musical activities, and dramatic play facilitates engaging in each of these. To allow ongoing project work and other age-appropriate activities, school-aged children should have separate areas. Materials should be appropriate for each age group and varied. Equipment/materials for sensory stimulation, manipulation, construction, active play, dramatic play, and books, recordings, and art supplies, all arranged for easy, independent child access and rotated for variety, are needed.

Arranging learning environments related to children's personal, privacy, and sensory needs
In any EC learning environment, the indoor space should include easily identifiable places where children and adults can store their personal belongings. Since EC involves children in groups for long time periods, they should be given indoor and outdoor areas allowing solitude and privacy while still easily permitting adult supervision. Playhouses and tunnels can be used outdoors, small interior rooms and partitions indoors. Environments should include softness in various forms like grass outdoors; carpet, pillows, and soft chairs indoors; adult laps to sit in and be cuddled; and soft play materials like clay, Play-Doh, finger paints, water, and sand. While noise is predictable, even desirable in EC environments, undue noise causing fatigue and stress should be controlled by noise-absorbing elements like rugs/carpets, drapes, acoustical ceilings and other building materials. Outdoor play areas supplied/arranged by school/community playgrounds should be separated from roadways and other hazards by fencing and/or natural barriers. Awnings can substitute for hills, and inclines/ramps for shade, when these are not naturally available. Surfaces and equipment should be varied.

Early childhood behavior management

Repetition and consistency are two major elements for managing young children's behavior. Adults must always follow and enforce whichever rules they designate. They must also remember that they will need to repeat their rules over and over to make them effective. Behaviorism has shown it is more powerful to reward good behaviors than punish bad behaviors. Consistently rewarding desired behaviors enables young children to make the association between behavior and reward. Functional behavior analysis can inform adults: knowing the function of a behavior is necessary to changing it. For example, if a toddler throws a tantrum out of frustration, providing support/scaffolding for a difficult task, breaking it down to more manageable increments via task analysis, and giving encouragement would be appropriate strategies; but if the tantrum was a bid for attention, adults would only reinforce/strengthen tantrum recurrence by paying attention. Feeling valued and loved within a positive relationship greatly supports young children's compliance with rules. The "10:1 Rule" prescribes at least 10 positive comments per 1 negative comment/correction.

Managing the normal behavior of young children

Before reacting to young children's behaviors, adults should make sure children understand the situation. They should state rules simply and clearly; repeat them frequently for a long time for young children to remember and follow them; and state and enforce rules very consistently to avoid confusion. Adults should tell children clearly what they expect of them. They should never assume they need do nothing when children follow rules; they should consistently give rewards for compliance. Adults should also explain to young children why they are/are not receiving rewards by citing the rule they did/did not follow. Adults can arrange the environment to promote success. For example, if a child throws things that break windows, adults can remove such objects and substitute softer/more lightweight items. Organization is also important. Adults should begin with a simple, easy-to-implement plan and adhere to it. They should record children's progress; analyzing the records shows what does/does not work and why, enabling new/revised plans.

Including families in children's education

First, ECE personnel can make sure that communication between the school/program and family is reciprocal and regular. EC educators should promote and support the enhancement and application of parenting skills. They should also acknowledge that parents have an integral part in supporting children's learning. All school personnel should make parents feel welcome in school, and moreover should seek parents' help and support. When school administrators, teachers, and other staff make educational decisions that affect the children and their families, they should always be sure that the children's parents are involved in these decisions. In addition, educational personnel should not just work on children's educational goals, learning objectives, and curricular and instructional planning and design on their own, keeping the school or program isolated; they should make use of all available community resources. Instead of trying to educate young children within a school bubble, educators who collaborate with their communities realize benefits of stronger families, schools, and child learning.

Flexibility and variety are key elements for involving diverse families, with changing situations and needs, in ECE. Adaptable approaches include these: Educators include families in designing children's Individual Family Service Plans (IFSPs) for preschoolers. They ask families to develop their own goals for educational participation. They create volunteer calendars, encouraging parents to collaborate when able. They communicate with families regularly, using speech if written/printed language presents barriers. They establish media libraries for parents/families to browse and check out resources. They facilitate parental meeting attendance and school visits by providing transportation and child care. They adapt to parental work schedules by convening meetings at alternative times of day. They often send families communications about both their children and class content, including information regarding important developmental milestones and methods for nurturing growth and development. They offer families individualized, specific strategies for home use. They recruit interested family members to help in preschool. They also function as clearinghouses to facilitate family access to community supports like local health care agencies, businesses, and universities.

Informal assessment instruments

EC teachers assess pre-K children's performance in individual, small-group, and whole-class activities throughout the day using informal tools that are teacher-made, school/program/district-furnished, or procured by school systems from commercial educational resources. For classroom observations, teachers might complete a form based on their observations during class story or circle time, organized using three themes per day, each targeting different skills—social-emotional, math, alphabet knowledge, oral language, or emergent writing. They note the names of children demonstrating the specified skill and those who might need follow-up, and provide needed one on one interventions daily. For individual observations, teachers might fill out a chart divided into domains like physical development; oral language development; math; emergent reading; emergent writing; science and health; fine arts; technology and media; social studies; social-emotional development; and approaches to learning, noting one child's strengths and needs in each area per chart. In addition to guided observation records, teachers complete checklists; keep anecdotal and running records; and assemble portfolio assessments of children's work. Tracking children's progress informs responsive instructional planning.

Formal assessment instruments

Formal assessment instruments are typically standardized tests, administered to groups. They give norms for age groups/developmental levels for comparison. They are designed to avoid administrator bias and capture children's responses only. Their data can be scaled and be reported in aggregate to school/program administrators and policymakers. The Scholastic Early Childhood Inventory (SECI) is a formal one on one instrument to assess children's progress in four domains found to predict kindergarten readiness: phonological awareness, oral language development, alphabet knowledge, and mathematics. Other instruments measuring multiple developmental domains include the Assessment, Evaluation and Programming System (0–6 years) for planning intervention; the Bayley Scale for Infant Development (1–42 months) for assessing developmental delays; the Brigance Diagnostic Inventory of Early Development (0–7 years) for planning instruction; the Developmental Profile II (0–6 years) to assess special needs and support IEP development; the Early Coping Inventory (4–36 months) and Early Learning Accomplishment Profile (0–36 months), both for planning interventions; and the Infant-Toddler Developmental Assessment (0–42 months) to screen for developmental delays.

Screening and assessment instruments

Differences among screening and assessment instruments
A variety of screening and assessment instruments exist for EC measurement. Some key areas where they differ include which developmental domains are measured by an instrument; for which applications an instrument is meant to be used; to which age ranges an instrument applies; the methods by which a test or tool is administered; the requirements for scoring and interpreting a test, scale, or checklist; whether an instrument is appropriate for use with ethnically diverse populations; and whether a tool is statistically found to have good validity and reliability. EC program administrators should choose instruments that can measure the developmental areas pertinent to their program; support their program's established goals; and include all EC ages served in their program. Instruments' administration, scoring, and interpretation methods should be congruent with program personnel's skills. Test/measure administration should involve realistic time

durations. Instruments/tools should be appropriate to use with ethnically diverse and non-English-speaking children and families. Tests should also be proven psychometrically accurate and dependable enough.

Typical applications of screening and assessment instruments

The ways in which screening and assessment instruments applicable to ECE are used include a wide range of variations. For example, ECE programs typically need to identify children who might have developmental disorders or delays. Screening instruments are used to identify those children showing signs of possible problems who need assessments, not to diagnose problems. Assessment instruments are used to develop and/or confirm diagnoses of developmental disorders or delays. Assessment tools are also used to help educators and therapists plan curricular and treatment programs. Another important function of assessment instruments is to determine a child's eligibility for a given program. In addition, once children are placed in ECE programs, assessment tools can be used to monitor their progress and other changes occurring through time. Moreover, program administrators can use assessment instruments to evaluate children's achievement of the learning outcomes that define their program goals—and by extension, the teachers' effectiveness in furthering children's achievement of those outcomes.

Measuring development by different screening and assessment instruments

The available screening and assessment instruments for EC development cover a wide range in scope and areas of focus. Some measures are comprehensive, assessing young children's progress in many developmental domains including sensory, motor, physical, cognitive, linguistic, emotional, and social. Some other instruments focus exclusively on only one domain, such as language development or emotional-social development. Some instruments even focus within a domain upon only one of its facets, e.g. upon attachment or temperament within the domain of emotional-social development. In addition, some tools measure risk and resiliency factors influencing developmental delays and disorders. Programs like Head Start that promote general EC development should select comprehensive assessment instruments. Outreach programs targeting better identification of children having untreated and/or undetected mental health problems should choose instruments assessing social-emotional development. Clinics treating children with regulatory disorders might select an instrument measuring temperament. Prevention programs helping multiple-needs families access supports and services could use a measure for risk and resiliency factors. Multifaceted EC programs often benefit most from using several instruments in combination.

Age ranges included in various screening and assessment instruments

An important consideration for screening and assessment in early childhood is that EC development is very dynamic and occurs rapidly. Hence screening and assessment instruments must be sensitive to such frequent and pronounced developmental changes. Some instruments target specific age ranges like 0–36 months. Others cover wider ranges, e.g. children aged 2–16 years. The latter may have internal means of application to smaller age ranges; for example, sections respectively for 3–6-month-old babies, 7–12-month-olds, and 12–18-month-olds. Or they indicate different scoring and interpretation criteria by age; for example, some screening tools specify different numbers of test items depending on the child's age to indicate a need for assessment. Choosing screening and assessment instruments covering the entire age range served in an ECE program is advantageous—not only because they can be used with all child ages in the program, but also because they can be administered and readministered at the beginning and end of programs and/or in between, to compare and monitor changes, which is difficult with separate, age-specific tests.

Scoring and interpretation of various screening and assessment instruments

Some instruments are fairly simple to score and interpret, needing little training of EC personnel. For example, paper-and-pencil questionnaires/surveys often only need the numbers/points for each item response added up for a total score; or a group of scores is obtained by summing values within sections. Interpreting some screening scores can be as simple as noting whether a child's score surpasses a designated cut-off value that signals assessment is needed. Such screenings can be scored and interpreted right after administration, and readily shared with parents and other stakeholders. Assessment instruments using more complicated scoring and interpretation include such procedures as weighting item values; reversing point values for certain items; converting raw scores into standardized scores or percentages; and referring to tables giving national norms for comparison. Standardized tests, including preschool IQ scales, commonly involve such methods. Assessors often need considerable training; advanced psychometric education and experience; thorough knowledge of EC development; and additional time to score and interpret these tests. Results may be discussed in separately scheduled meetings.

Screening and assessment tools that use structured tasks

Screening and assessment instruments that use structured tasks involve a list of behaviors and/or skills that a child is expected to attain by a certain age range or developmental level. The administrators must present various activities or tasks to a child, and then record the details of the child's performance of each activity or task. Instruments using structured tasks require EC staff training for administration. They take over 20 minutes to complete. EC programs/schools/agencies must buy testing equipment/materials and single-use recording forms. Because paper-and-pencil questionnaires/surveys are easy to administer; apply across various settings, e.g. preschools, pediatricians' waiting rooms, homes, etc.; cost comparatively little; require minimal administrator training; and are frequently short, they are appropriate for screening use. While formal/informal observational tools, structured/semistructured interview tools, and structured-task tools take more training, time, and expense, they also provide more detailed information, making them useful for determining diagnoses and/or developing individualized care/instruction plans. Instruments using multiple methods, e.g. collecting data from various settings and respondents, yield the most comprehensive information.

Formal and informal observations

Some instruments require EC staff to watch a child's behavior and/or interactions with parents/caregivers and/or peers. Formal observations involve watching activities structured for the screening/assessment instrument. Informal observations involve watching a child's activities in natural settings like at home or in preschool during play times. Formal observation tools typically require staff to be trained to administer them. The trained observers' findings can include records of which developmentally normal behaviors a child has attained, incidences of problem behaviors noted, descriptions and evaluations of the quality of a child's social interactions with other people, and other observations of the child's behaviors that can inform screening and assessment. Observational screening and assessment instruments usually take more than 20 minutes for administration. Publishers of observational tests typically charge EC programs to order single-use recording forms; some allow them to purchase templates and then reproduce the forms.

Paper-and-pencil reports

The most common form of paper-and-pencil report about infants and young children are questionnaires. Parents, caregivers, and teachers read printed questions or statements and respond by selecting Yes or No to a question or a number/level on a Likert-type scale showing the degree to which they agree with a statement. For self-administration, instruments must contain questions/statements written on reading levels accessible to the respondents and in their native languages. Alternatively, some questionnaires or surveys can be read to the respondent by an interviewer trained in or familiar with administration of the chosen instrument. Such self-reporting instruments usually take fewer than 20 minutes to finish, and ECE program personnel need comparatively little training to administer them. However, employees may need further training to score and/or interpret responses, or already-trained specialists may score and interpret them in some cases. ECE schools/programs/agencies can obtain some self-reporting instruments free of charge; other tools' publishers charge for response forms; and others charge only for initially obtaining their materials, allowing purchasers to reproduce them thereafter.

Interviews

In EC programs conducting assessments, personnel usually conduct interviews with a child's parents, teachers, and/or caregivers. Interviews can be made in structured formats, i.e. the administrator reads prescribed questions as written to the interviewee, or semi-structured formats, wherein the administrator uses his/her judgment to add more questions to the written ones until s/he determines that the information provided is complete enough. Interview questions vary, covering subjects of parental concern, the child's identified areas of strengths and accomplishments, the child's identified areas of deficits or needs, the interactions between parents and child, and the child's behavior. Interviews can be brief, but usually they are longer than paper-and-pencil self-reporting questionnaires, surveys, or checklists. EC personnel frequently need to be trained to administer published interview-based instruments. Publishers typically charge schools/programs/agencies for ordering multiple, single-use response forms, or they may require a one-time order and allow them to reproduce the forms from their initial purchase to use for multiple administrations.

Test-retest reliability

Test-retest reliability is how consistent/stable an instrument's results are across administrations. An instrument with good test-retest reliability yields the same results when administered twice or more to the same child within a short time. For example, the same assessor gives a child the same test twice within a few days or weeks, comparing the results. The more similar the results between/among administrations, the higher the test-retest reliability. This implies the instrument measures an attribute/construct that is stable over a short time. Due to the inherent rapidity and dynamism of EC development, we expect significant developmental changes over years and months; but over only weeks or days, we expect little or no substantial change. Therefore, instruments whose results are not stable over a short time are less utile for EC screening/assessment. For example, a child's scoring with "typical development" on one administration but "possible delay/disorder" a week later means the instrument does not define the child's developmental needs, and thus is not reliable.

Inter-rater reliability

Inter-rater reliability is how consistent/stable an instrument's results are across different individual administrators/raters. Good inter-rater reliability means the instrument will give the same/similar results for the same child, at the same time, in the same setting, when administered by different people. This shows that the instrument measures a quality/construct that remains stable regardless of who administers the test. Significant differences among different raters' results present problems, especially with instruments using unstructured interviews, observations, or structured tasks. For example, if one rater scores a child as possibly having a developmental delay or disorder while another rater using the same test scores the same child as within the range of normal development, the instrument does not identify the child's true developmental needs and is unreliable. When different assessors (like parent vs. teacher) observe a child in different settings, though, like home vs. preschool, and/or at different times, varying results are expected and not necessarily indicative of inter-rater unreliability because children's behaviors can vary by setting.

Internal consistency

A testing instrument is said to have internal consistency when its individual items correlate strongly with each other and with the total test score. This means that all of the individual items (questions, stimuli, tasks, etc.) measure parts of the same construct that the test is intended to measure. A test with low internal consistency could be measuring additional attributes that the authors did not define or mean for the test to measure. Children with disparate developmental needs could thus receive similar scores, based on different test items. With comprehensive screening and assessment instruments that cover multiple domains of development, EC educators should look for internal consistency within each subscale of the test or within each domain tested. However, they should not necessarily expect internal consistency among the different domains or at the level of the test's full-scale/overall score. For example, they should not expect high correlation between a test's subscale measuring a child's language skills development and its subscale measuring a child's gross motor skills development.

Concurrent validity

When a screening or assessment instrument yields results comparable to those of another instrument whose validity has been previously established, it has good concurrent validity. Since the test used for comparison was already found valid, users have confidence in its results. Therefore, their confidence is warranted in another test showing high concurrent validity with the established test. For example, the Stanford-Binet Intelligence Scales and the Wechsler Preschool and Primary Scales of Intelligence (WPPSI) are both well-established IQ tests with demonstrated statistical validity and reliability. So if EC educators have found or been given a new instrument for measuring intelligence, they are likely to find that its authors have compared the test's results to the results obtained by the Stanford-Binet and/or WPPSI. Educators who have confidence in the Stanford-Binet and/or the WPPSI are then justified in having comparable confidence in the new test if its results were found similar to those of the established tests, indicating its high concurrent validity.

Content validity

Whether a test instrument measures the entire content area it purports to measure is known as content validity. It determines whether a test can yield accurate and fair measures of the totality of the construct that the assessor wants to test. For example, if a screening instrument is intended to measure social-emotional development in a young child, it should include individual test items covering the range of this domain's important components. A screening test that covers a child's interactions with caregivers but not with peers; screens attention but not initiation of play; or screens for social skills but not communication skills would not address all elements of social-emotional development and thus not have good content validity. EC educators can use instruments with high content validity to generalize with more confidence about how a child's test performance predicts his/her levels of functioning in real life. By contrast, if a test has low content validity, generalizations about the tested child's development can exceed the test's scope and be inaccurate and/or unrealistic.

Predictive validity

A screening/assessment instrument's prediction of a child's behavior in real life is predictive validity. For example, an instrument screening for social-emotional disorders in preschool children might predict tantrum and/or oppositional behaviors in kindergarten. In another example, you would expect a screening instrument for social-emotional disorders to differentiate between children with normal/typical social-emotional development and those with mental health disorders. If a screening tool identifies a child with a potential mental health disorder and has high predictive validity, a complete clinical diagnostic evaluation of the screened child would diagnose a mental health disorder. Sensitivity is the instrument's accuracy—here, in identifying developmental disorders/delays, if it correctly identifies 9 of 10 children really having disorders/delays, it has 90 percent sensitivity. Specificity conversely would be accuracy in identifying children without disorders/delays. Despite high sensitivity and specificity, screeners yield some errors. False-positives over-identify delays/disorders where none exist; false-negatives under-identify existing delays/disorders. Unnecessary concern is a consequence of false-positives; lack of prevention/early intervention/treatment is a more serious consequence of false-negatives.

Internal consistency

Whether a test's individual items contribute to measuring the construct the test is supposed to measure is internal consistency. It is determined by how much the test's individual items correlate with one another and with the overall score. A test with high internal consistency more accurately measures the specific content area/developmental domain/construct it means to measure. A test with low internal consistency poses problems when children who might have very different needs get the same score. For example, if a test meant to measure aggression has low internal consistency, its individual items are not correlated with one another or the overall score, implying it tests more than one construct. Two children given this test could score beyond the cutoff level indicating diagnosis or assessment need, but their scores could be due to completely different individual test items. Since individual test items do not correlate, the two children might have markedly different needs. Furthermore, those needs may not be related to aggression, since the test probably unintentionally measures additional constructs.

Norm-referenced versus criterion-referenced tests

Norm-referenced tests compare a child's test results to those of a comparison group of other children in the same age group, grade, or developmental level. This comparison group is called a normative or standardization sample. Norm-referenced tests show how an individual child's performance compares to that of the general population of children. Criterion-referenced tests compare a child's test results to a predetermined standard of performance for the child's age group/grade/level. They show how an individual child's performance compares to standards established by educational experts. Norm-referenced tests are useful for determining whether a child is similar to the "average" child and identifying children performing significantly above or below average. Criterion-referenced tests are good for measuring the extent to which an individual child has mastered areas or domains of development and for monitoring changes over time in the child's levels of mastery.

Elements of applying assessment results to planning instruction

ECE settings should provide organized outlines of developmentally appropriate guidelines for their children, including when and how to introduce and reinforce guidelines at each learning stage. These outlines are foundations for anecdotal observations and authentic assessments tracking developmental progress. ECE programs supply opportunities and activities to develop each discrete skill, including copious review and practice young children require for retention. Teachers should plan learning experiences meaningfully promoting developing identified guidelines and addressing children's interests. ECE settings should have organized progress-tracking systems following developmental sequences. These help teachers determine whether a child can move to the next level or prior skills that need additional reinforcement. Tracking systems should be easy to maintain and immediately give teachers basic information regarding each child's level of functioning for planning activities and discussions. Teachers should then create "ready reference" charts/graphs of assessment and monitoring results, giving an idea of the class/group's general functioning level, to inform activity/lesson planning and additional support needed for individual children—one on one for those below class/group level, enriched for those above it.

Good communication with children's parents

When teachers send home a letter to parents explaining classroom practices and giving contact information at the beginning of the school year, parents perceive them as approachable and available. When a teacher calls each parent/guardian during school's first two weeks, parents appreciate and enjoy conversations. Calls also make it easier for teachers to contact parents later in the year regarding child issues if needed. Experts find it effective to mail postcards home, addressed to children or parents. Establishing simple class websites including teacher contact information facilitates parental access. Teachers' printing business cards and attaching them to their first parent letters conveys professionalism. Teachers using Internet/e-mail/print to publish weekly/monthly class newsletters informally keep parents apprised of children's instruction and teach parents to expect communication. Teachers can send parents invitations to visit prior to school/program Open Houses: teachers are perceived as more approachable when more parents are comfortable in classrooms. Having children write appreciation letters to parents for Open Houses encourages children to invite parents; parents also perceive teacher appreciation by association.

Professionalism

Professionalism and professional responsibility

While care and instruction of young children are delivered through a variety of program types, EC educators share common general goals. They appreciate EC as a unique period in life. They work to educate holistically, considering the mind, feelings, and body of the whole child. The educational goals they develop are designed to support each child's fulfilling his/her individual potential within relationship contexts. EC professionals realize children are inseparable from their social milieus of family, society, and culture; they work to relate to and understand children in these contexts, while also appreciating and supporting family ties. They apply their knowledge of child development, teaching according to how children learn and what they need, and apply research in the field to differentiating common assumptions and myths from valid scientific findings. They have appropriate behavioral expectations for children at each developmental stage. EC professionals realize the significance of confidentiality: they never gossip or tell families personal information about other families. Lifelong learners, they set their own professional goals, pursuing ongoing professional development.

Legal responsibilities of EC professionals

Historically, special education was introduced with the purpose of separating special-needs children from their normally developing peers. However, since 1991, the IDEA legislation has established the necessity of inclusion in normal care and educational environments, including EC settings, for children with disabilities. EC professionals know excluding any child is illegal. Another example of legal responsibilities is the "mandated reporter" status of caregivers/teachers/other adults working with children and families. They are legally required to report suspected child abuse and neglect; the law penalizes them for not reporting. For example, an EC teacher sees injuries to a child. S/he knows the mother has a new boyfriend, displays a fearful attitude, and responds evasively to teacher questions. Later, the child tells the teacher the boyfriend hurt him/her. The teacher pities the mother, realizing she needs the boyfriend financially and emotionally, and reporting suspected abuse could make the mother lose her children or their home. Regardless, the teacher must report suspicions by law, which was enacted for stopping violence against children.

Interactions with other adults in the learning environment

Regarding teachers' roles, much of the focus is on observing children and their behaviors, helping children manage peer interactions, and giving children opportunities for developing peer-group social skills. Too often a similar emphasis is not accorded to teachers' reflecting on their interactions and behaviors with other adults; learning to collaborate with other adults; and developing skills for conflict resolution and managing disagreements with other adults. Some experts say teachers should work diligently and deliberately to make adult interactions integral parts of daily classroom activity. For group ECE settings to attain their goals, adults must make and implement plans collaboratively. However, mandatory staff meetings are commonly occupied with curricular and administrative requirements; beyond these, little or no attention or time is applied to nurturing adult-adult relationships. Adults interact during in-service trainings and professional development experiences, but outside of daily classroom settings. Nevertheless, these experiences can be used as foundations for better adult-adult communication within ECE contexts. Conscious efforts to develop adult-adult relationships benefiting children's growth, development, and learning are necessary.

Enabling and supporting positive interactions among adults within the ECE setting

Adults engage in positive interactions with each other within ECE programs when they make time to share their anecdotal records and observations of their young students, and collaboratively plan instruction based on their collective contributions. When adults share information and communicate with one another about the children and their families with whom they work, they interact positively together. When EC educators engage in problem-solving activities and dialogues, these help them identify which learning goals and experiences they can make more effective for the children and how they can do this. Adults within ECE settings should engage in reciprocal exchanging of ideas about the EC learning environment and about how to share responsibilities for performing instructional tasks, rearranging classrooms as needed, setting up class projects, taking care of class pets and plants, and other such daily duties.

Adult-adult interactions

Addressing in research and theoretical literature and professional development
ECE research contains little work addressing adults' cooperation and collaborative expertise with each other and the influences of these on children. However, the High/Scope curriculum model, The Creative Curriculum, and similar curriculum models and approaches do address adult-adult interactions by stressing how important teamwork is in planning lessons and sharing responsibilities and information. In addition, some educational experts have written about power struggles and other interactional dynamics in adult-adult relationships that can impede employee performance in a variety of settings. Professional development and training programs rarely include adult conflict-resolution techniques, instruction in working collaboratively, or adult learning principles. Hence educators must consider how their adult-adult interactions can support children's development of competence, capability, and confidence. Sharing instructional goals, planning learning experiences that support goals, and sharing responsibilities as a team for implementing projects establishes climates of safety and trust for children.

Applying the concept of "quality time" to interactions

Educators have noted that attitudes and things we commonly say to children, e.g. "Your actions speak louder than your words" would equally benefit us addressing our own behaviors as adults. Applying the same principles we teach children to interactions among adults in the learning community can positively influence those interactions, which in turn affects adult-child/teacher-student interactions and overall classroom atmospheres. Without such atmospheres conducive to trust and honesty in adult relationships, educators can fall prey to misunderstandings and internalizing negative attitudes, which influence not only coworker interactions but moreover classroom climates. One solution is for adults in ECE to establish occasions affording "quality adult time." Psychotherapist and psychological theorist Virginia Satir, pioneer of family therapy, found interpersonal dynamics influenced by positive adult-adult communication. Trust-building, mutual colleague support, and sharing experiences/feelings—related or unrelated to classrooms—promote adult relationships that benefit teacher-learner relationships and thus enhance young children's development and learning.

Confidentiality of records

In EC settings, records kept about children and their families must be treated with strict confidentiality. EC centers/programs/preschools/agencies should limit access to student records to children's immediate family members; only those employees authorized; and agencies having legal authority to access records. Confidentiality of records and restricted access to them in all centers/programs/preschools/agencies that receive federal funding are mandated by the Family Educational Rights and Privacy Act (FERPA). Moreover, with the ongoing trend toward educational inclusion, many EC settings serve children with disabilities, whose student records are additionally subject to regulations under the federal Individuals with Disabilities Education Act (IDEA), and also to the special education laws of their respective U.S. states. An exception to the laws regarding records confidentiality is mandated reporting by EC personnel of suspected child abuse and neglect. Laws applying to child abuse and neglect supersede FERPA regulations. Legally, EC employees are both required to report suspected abuse and neglect of children, and immune from liability for releasing child records information relevant to their reporting.

Legal issues relative to economic considerations

To furnish and sustain quality care in EC settings is always challenging to care providers. It is even more so during difficult economic times. Many EC centers must face decisions whether to downsize the services they offer or to go out of business. When administrators choose to remain in operation, they encounter equally difficult decisions regarding how to reduce services, but not at the expense of quality. A legal issue related to such economic considerations is that EC personnel are often placed at legal risk when service quality is compromised. While EC employers, employees, young children's parents, and educational researchers are all interested in and pursue a definition of quality care, no single operational definition has been attained. However, EC professionals with ample work experience in EC centers have contributed various definitions. The consensus of their contributions includes the following common elements: a nurturing environment; employees trained in EC development and methods; age-appropriate curricula; sufficient space, equipment, and materials; safety and good maintenance of physical environments; and good parent-teacher communication.

Medical care and treatment

The child care licensing regulations of each U.S. state government mostly govern children's medical care and treatment in EC settings. Overall, state regulations emphasize four areas of medical care and treatment: (1) Health requirements for all employees, such as having no communicable diseases; passing a TB test; having no health conditions preventing active child care; and maintaining accurate employee as well as child health records; (2) Administration by staff of medication to children being served in EC settings; (3) Management by EC staff of emergencies due to illness, injury, and accidents; and (4) Treatment of nonemergency minor illnesses, injuries, and accidents occurring to children in EC settings. To protect children's health and safety, EC programs/schools/centers must maintain written policies and procedures for emergency and nonemergency care. To protect personnel from litigation, they must adhere scrupulously to written policies and procedures. Litigation for damages/injury is likely when not following procedures. Not reporting suspected/observed child abuse/neglect and not completing accident reports also invite lawsuits.

Non-emergency medical illnesses

EC programs must keep procedures for, and reports on, non-emergency medical treatment of children on file just as they do for emergency procedures and reporting. Staff must contact and notify a sick child's parents, who decide if the child should leave the center/preschool. If so, parents should transport their child. Parental consent forms should authorize a doctor or nurse to provide routine medical treatment. EC centers/preschools should have sick children wait to be picked up in a location that is separate from other children and activities, but closely supervised by staff. For children with allergies, diabetes, and other chronic medical conditions, EC centers/preschools should not only keep this information on file in records, but also post it accessibly at all times for staff reference. Instructions for any special treatment should be included. For any health impairment(s) a child has that could potentially involve emergency treatment, directions for staff should be visibly posted, including specific employees designated to administer treatment. This protects children from harm and caregivers/educators from legal liability.

Medical emergencies

For a child's non-life-threatening medical emergencies, EC personnel should request transportation by the child's parents. However, if parents cannot transport the child, or in a more severe emergency, EC administrators should call an ambulance. In life-threatening emergencies that preclude waiting for an ambulance, EC administrators must designate the vehicle and responsible employee for transporting the child to the hospital; this information should be posted in the facility's emergency procedures. Administrators should keep the number of staff involved in emergency medical treatment to a minimum. Those employees they designate for involvement should be willing to take on the responsibility and should have current first aid training. The administrators can include a clause in these employees' job descriptions providing for their transporting children in the event of an emergency. The EC facility may also pay for additional or separate liability insurance coverage of the employees they designate as responsible for providing necessary emergency medical treatment.

Administration of medication

The administration of medication to children in EC settings has been subject to much controversy due to obvious issues of dangers and liability. EC centers/programs must write their policies and procedures to include their state government's licensing requirements for medical care and treatment, which they must follow closely. Experts recommend that parent and doctor permission be required for administering any prescription and nonprescription medications to children. EC settings should keep on file written parental consent for each medication, and review these records regularly for changes. They should also post separate charts, easily accessible to staff, with each child's name, medication, dosage, administration time, and teacher initials. These provide documentation of teachers following parent directions and can prevent mistakes. Staff should label all medications with the drug name, child's name, doctor's name and contact information, and administration instructions. EC centers seasonally and frequently contain many children simultaneously recovering from a variety of illnesses; labeling prevents giving children the wrong medication. Empty drug containers should be returned to parents.

Emergency medical treatment and first aid

EC programs and preschools must write specific, detailed procedures regarding emergency treatment and keep these on file. Children's parents, EC administrators, and EC staff need to be informed regarding what will occur in the event of a child's serious illness or injury. EC settings must also keep written, signed parental consent forms on file, as well as parent contact information, parental physician and hospital preferences, and health insurance information. EC staff should have current, regularly updated first aid training. First aid equipment should be stored in locations accessible to personnel, who should be frequently reminded of these locations. Lists of each staff member's first aid responsibilities and training should be posted, also accessibly. Licensing regulations require EC facilities to notify parents of emergencies; not doing so is subject to legal action. In non-life-threatening emergencies, staff should ask parents to furnish transportation and medical treatment. For grave emergencies, parental consent forms should be filed and updated semi-annually, including physician and hospital names, ambulance service, and other transportation procedures.

Custody issues

EC facilities are affected by two types of issues involving child custody: (1) Parents are pursuing legal and/or physical custody of the child but they are not living together; and (2) State authorities have removed a child from the parents' legal and physical custody. Parents frequently demand the right to visit with and/or take the child home on occasion. Two types of custody are: legal custody, defined as an individual's or agency's right to make decisions on a child's behalf regarding the child's place of residence, medical treatment, and education; and physical custody, defined as an individual's or agency's right and responsibility to provide a child with immediate care, and a household or care facility for the present and immediate future. Physical custody does not include all of the rights of full legal custody. It is serious for a child to be in the middle of a custody battle between divorcing parents or between parents and foster parents; therefore EC facilities need the most concise, clear-cut guidelines possible.

Recommendations to follow pertaining to custody
It is recommended that during a child's enrollment, EC programs procure a signed, dated document clarifying the child's custody status, including names, contact information, and relationships of all individuals authorized to pick up the child. Copies of any separation agreement/court decree should also be filed. Any time EC staff do not recognize an individual coming to pick up a child, they should ask the person to produce photo identification, which they should closely inspect. EC program administrators cannot make decisions regarding who has legal or physical custody of a child they serve. When a parent or other adult enrolls a child in an EC program, that adult is asked to list other persons to be contacted in the event of an emergency. EC administrators are advised to present all parents/guardians with a statement that the EC center will only release their child to someone the enrolling parent/adult listed on the emergency form as authorized to pick up the child.

Non-custodial or non-authorized adults attempting to pick up children
EC centers should always have up-to-date documentation on file of a child's custodial arrangements, signed and dated by the enrolling adult. If an adult not authorized to pick up the child attempts to do so, an EC administrator should inform that adult of the center's policies and procedures regarding custody. They may even show the unauthorized adult their copy of the custodial court order if needed. If the unauthorized adult then departs, the administrator must notify the enrolling adult of the incident; file a written report of it; meet with the custodial adult to clarify custody arrangements anew; document this meeting, including its date and signatures; and file the document in the child's record. If the

unauthorized adult refuses to leave and makes a scene or threatens/displays violence, the EC administrator should call the police if needed. The EC center's having a procedure in place for protecting children against emotionally upsetting scenes and/or violent adult behavior is crucial to the children's safety and well-being.

Children not picked up timely by parents/designated others

If a child is not picked up on time from an EC center at the end of its defined day, the EC center has the legal responsibility for the child's welfare as long as the child is on the premises. In the event that a child is left at the EC center for a long time and the parent/authorized adult has not notified the center why and/or when the child will be picked up, EC personnel are advised that keeping the child at the center is less likely to incur legal liability than for the child to stay at an EC staff member's home, for example. If the child has to be removed, it is important for EC staff to inform the police of this and where they are taking the child. If parents are chronically tardy picking up children, EC staff should review the child's information and/or inquire further of parents to ascertain reasons and possible solutions because they are legally responsible for reporting suspected child neglect.

Practice Test

Practice Questions

1. A teacher asks her students to compare and contrast two animals they saw at the zoo. This is an example of what level of Bloom's taxonomy?
    a. Knowledge
    b. Comprehension
    c. Application
    d. Analysis

2. Students studying fractions manipulate "fraction blocks," blocks cut to represent fractional parts, to learn the concept of adding and subtracting fractions. Which level of development as described by Piaget does this activity demonstrate?
    a. Sensory-motor stage
    b. Pre-operational stage
    c. Concrete operational stage
    d. Formal operations stage

3. According to Kohlberg, at which developmental level do children understand that good behavior is expected?
    a. Post-Conventional
    b. Conventional
    c. Pre-Conventional
    d. Adolescent

4. Erikson's stages of development include all of the following except
    a. Young childhood
    b. Middle adulthood
    c. Adolescence
    d. Late childhood

5. In Bronfenbrenner's organization of child development, the family or classroom is considered a
    a. Chronosystem
    b. Microsystem
    c. Macrosystem
    d. Mesosystem

6. One of Vygotsky's major contributions to the field of early childhood development is the concept of
    a. Punishment/obedience
    b. A taxonomy of learning skill levels
    c. The importance of play as a learning activity
    d. The formal operations stage of development

7. Which of the following is a component of the Constructivist learning theory?
   a. Students, teachers, and classmates establish knowledge cooperatively every day
   b. Students are taught to develop skills in problem solving and critical thinking
   c. Children only learn language and culture through interaction with adults and other children
   d. It is important to help the learner gain an understanding of how knowledge is constructed

8. Social and behavioral theories of learning stress the importance of
   a. Good behavior on the part of students
   b. The social interactions of students that aid or inhibit learning
   c. A reward system for good behavior or growth in skills
   d. The direct connection between thoughts and speech

9. A teacher becomes aware that a certain student's family is in a crisis situation. What is his or her best course of action?
   a. Counsel the child on how best to handle the situation at home
   b. Contact the parents with a direct offer to help with their problems
   c. Report the crisis situation to school or civil authorities
   d. Attempt to deal with the student as well as possible despite the situation

10. Which of the following is the best way to assist children from families with limited incomes?
   a. Lower expectations for these children's achievements in the classroom
   b. Cooperate with school administrators and public officials to provide such assistance as a free lunch program and/or some academic assistance
   c. Counsel parents on ways to economize with their limited financial resources
   d. Provide the best possible instruction without any need for intervention or public assistance

11. The teacher notices that a student's attention in the classroom is decreased. The student seems restless and unable to concentrate. Which of the following may be the cause of this change in behavior?
   a. The child is coming down with an illness, such as the flu
   b. A problem has developed at home, such as divorce or abuse
   c. The child has entered a period of rapid physical growth which distracts him or her from cognitive activity
   d. All or any of the above

12. Which of the following is a symptom of an emotionally-neglected child?
   a. Extreme focus on school activities, seeking self-esteem
   b. Acts of jealousy or aggression toward other children
   c. Cooperative attitude in the classroom and on the playground
   d. Initiating social interaction with other students in the class at inappropriate times

13. Which of the following is an important aspect of allowing and encouraging children's play?
    a. Children need frequent opportunities to rest and relax
    b. Play teaches children cooperation and sharing
    c. Play encourages competition and opposition
    d. Play time gives the teacher a much needed rest period

14. What personal benefits can a young child obtain from play?
    a. Development of motor skills, such as hand-eye coordination
    b. Development of personal interests
    c. The ability to entertain himself or herself when alone
    d. All of the above

15. Social development and cognitive development often progress together because
    a. The more knowledge a child has, the more social he becomes
    b. As children are developing physically, they lose interest in social interactions
    c. Children develop the dexterity to show their cognitive development
    d. All areas of development—physical, social, and cognitive—are interrelated

16. The concept of latent development is important for teachers because:
    a. Teachers can be more patient with students if they understand their latency
    b. Teachers can wait until a student demonstrates complete ability in a certain skill area
    c. Teachers will be able to instruct the class as a whole group if they understand the stage at which everyone in the classroom is developing
    d. Developing skills may give clues for the next stage of instruction a student will need

17. A flat or agitated expression coupled with incoherent speech is a major symptom of
    a. Autism
    b. Drug or alcohol abuse
    c. Schizophrenia
    d. Intellectual disabilities

18. Which of the following actions are important for a teacher to do to create learning conditions for students with disabilities?
    a. Use a child-centered approach to instruction
    b. Help students identify their own learning needs
    c. Structure learning experiences appropriate to the needs of the disabled student
    d. All of the above

19. When a child begins to act violently, breaking things and quarreling with other students, teachers should see this change in behavior as a
    a. Sign of intellectual disabilities
    b. Sign of emotional difficulties
    c. Sign the child is becoming autistic
    d. Sign the child is abusing drugs or alcohol

Copyright © Mometrix Media. You have been licensed one copy of this document for personal use only. Any other reproduction or redistribution is strictly prohibited. All rights reserved.

20. If a child exhibits loss in cognitive thinking, social behavior, and usual academic progress, the teacher should suspect that the child
    a. May be developing schizophrenia
    b. May be having emotional problems at home
    c. May be epileptic
    d. May be abusing drugs

21. What makes a child eligible for special education services?
    a. Falling behind academically and refusing to do any work at school
    b. Having a diagnosed physical or emotional disability that has been evaluated professionally
    c. Recommendation by the classroom teacher that the child needs additional help
    d. Request by parents for the child to be given special education services

22. If a child demonstrates a lack of concentration in the classroom and also becomes easily agitated, he or she may be suffering from
    a. Lack of sleep and/or nutrition
    b. Little verbal interaction at home
    c. A significant mental or emotional disability
    d. Severe physical abuse

23. The statement, "a pencil is to an essay as a skillet is to food" is an example of:
    a. Metaphor
    b. Simile
    c. Symbolism
    d. Repetition

24. If a child appears delayed in speech development, which of the following is the best course to follow?
    a. Take a wait-and-see approach, as there are wide variations in patterns of speech development
    b. Use in-depth evaluations and early intervention to assist the child with language delays
    c. Help the child with common developmental speech problems, such as saying "w" for "r"
    d. Have the child repeat common words and phrases after an adult pronounces them

25. Which of the following is NOT a characteristic of a child with emotional disturbance?
    a. Lower academic performance
    b. Social skills deficits
    c. Aggressive behaviors
    d. Exaggerated efforts to make friends

26. How should the teacher best deal with an academically talented student who typically finishes work ahead of other students and tends to get into mischief while waiting for others to finish?
   a. Reprimand the student and remind him or her that his talents require setting a good example.
   b. Assign the student an appealing task related to the subject area that requires creativity, research, and/or in-depth study of the subject, such as creating a play or making a collage
   c. Permit the early finisher to have additional play time or extended recess as a reward for rapid completion of assignments
   d. Have the student tutor or help those who are not finished because they are having difficulty with the assignment

27. The most important factor for the teacher to keep in mind when teaching students with disabilities is
   a. Vary instructional pace and content to meet the specific needs of disabled students
   b. Slow the pace of classroom instruction to give the disabled students time to catch up
   c. Group the disabled students into a special section set apart from the regular students
   d. Insist that disabled students remain in their seats and focus on instruction

28. Seeking the appropriate method for meeting the needs of a disabled student is most often initiated by
   a. Parents
   b. A school's Child Study Team
   c. Community agencies
   d. The student's classroom teacher

29. Involvement of parents in developing a student's IEP (individualized education program) is essential because:
   a. An IEP must be approved by a parent before it can be enacted
   b. Parents know their children's needs, and an IEP must be tailored to those needs
   c. Teachers do not have the legal rights to discuss student needs with community representatives
   d. Students will not be willing to follow an IEP unless they have parental support

30. What is meant by the "least restrictive environment" policy of the IDEA?
   a. It is permissible to retain disabled students without passing them to the next grade level
   b. Students with disabilities need to be instructed in special classes
   c. Students with disabilities must be educated in an environment appropriate to them and their non-disabled peers, often a regular classroom
   d. Disabled students must be permitted to participate in the same classroom instruction as their non-disabled peers, even when it does not quite meet their needs

31. An IEP is a plan for
   a. Providing a tutor for an educationally handicapped student
   b. Providing counseling for an emotionally disturbed student
   c. Assisting parents in their problems handling a disabled student
   d. Assisting students in ways beyond what the classroom teacher can provide

32. A 504 differs from an IEP in that the 504
   a. Focuses on helping emotionally or physically disabled students within the classroom
   b. Is a legal document and requires formal assessment of the disability
   c. Requires the student to be referred for help by a parent or family member
   d. Requires regular monitoring and may be adjusted during the school year

33. Which of the following is NOT a reason for having a parent conference?
   a. The teacher wants to share information about the child's behavior and progress with the parents
   b. The teacher wants to receive information about the child from the parents
   c. The teacher wants to ask for parent support or involvement in specific activities
   d. The child's behavior is so difficult that the teacher wants the parents to withdraw the child from school

34. What is the advantage of placing students in community organizations like the ASB (Associated Student Body) or the PTSA (Parent Teacher Student Association)?
   a. These organizations help students to become politically savvy and be able to manipulate the rules of their school
   b. These organizations help students who are falling behind in school with tutoring and mentoring
   c. These organizations provide opportunities for students to develop leadership skills and learn to appreciate the value of collaborative processes
   d. Membership in these organizations can be listed on a student resume when the student is applying to colleges or universities

35. Which of the following genres is most important for children just beginning to become readers in grades K, 1, and 2?
   a. Alphabet books, wordless picture books, and easy-to-read books
   b. Legends and tall tales
   c. Biographies and informational books
   d. Chapter books and fantasy books

36. Which of the following is NOT a goal of children's literature?
   a. Focus on choices, morals, and values
   b. Instruct students through entertaining stories
   c. Promote an interest in reading itself
   d. Instruct students in the sciences, such as mathematics and biology

37. In which genre does the literature rely on the reader's suspension of disbelief about magical and mythical creatures?
   a. Science fiction
   b. Fantasy
   c. Action and adventure
   d. Historical fiction

38. A story about a young detective who solves mysteries using mental and physical skills would be classified as
    a. Action and adventure
    b. Historical fiction
    c. Horror and ghost stories
    d. Biography

39. The statement, "He ran away like a startled rabbit," is an example of
    a. Simile
    b. Metaphor
    c. Symbolism
    d. Repetition

40. Young children are more likely to respond to analogies in stories than to metaphors because
    a. They are old enough to understand the abstract thinking and symbolism that analogies express
    b. The ability to understand the kinds of abstraction expressed in metaphors is not developed until later in childhood
    c. They can apply the concepts expressed in analogies to their own daily lives, but metaphors do not compare things that children are familiar with
    d. Metaphors and symbols are usually found only in books that children find boring because of their abstractions

41. When students compare nonfiction literature to fictional literature, what differences will they find?
    a. Nonfiction stories will be told in logical order and will relate only the facts, while fictional stories are never told in logical order
    b. Fictional stories deal with plot, characters, setting, and themes, and nonfiction does not
    c. In addition to plot, character, setting, and theme, a nonfiction work will also introduce interpretations, theory, and research
    d. Students will find few, if any, differences between these two types of literature because they are essentially the same

42. Which of the following would you expect children in grades k–2 to learn by being exposed to both fictional and nonfictional literature?
    a. How to tell fiction from nonfiction
    b. How to do research to find information
    c. How to tell if a nonfiction writer is writing from a biased viewpoint
    d. How to understand themes, theories, and settings

43. In selecting literature for children, the most important first step a teacher should perform is to evaluate
    a. Whether the characters are interesting
    b. Whether the plots are appealing
    c. Class composition and preferences
    d. The reading level of the material

44. What is the best way for a teacher to make sure that books in the classroom are at an appropriate reading level, neither too easy nor so difficult that beginning readers will become frustrated?
    a. Administer a reading pretest to the class before selecting suitable books
    b. Purchase books that are easy enough for even the most beginning of readers
    c. Make sure that all the books are just slightly above students' reading level, so they will grow
    d. Provide a wide variety of reading materials for children to choose from

45. One of the most important elements in children's literature that captures children's interest is
    a. Character
    b. Accuracy
    c. Information
    d. Vocabulary

46. If a teacher does not have time to pre-read all the books she selects for her classroom, what is a good alternative?
    a. Look at children's book reviews in professional materials
    b. Seek input from children themselves about their favorite books
    c. Seek the assistance of the school librarian
    d. All of the above

47. The adaptation of language in a piece of writing to meet the author's purpose or audience is called
    a. Theme
    b. Point of view
    c. Style
    d. Voice

48. The perspective from which a story is told is called
    a. Theme
    b. Point of view
    c. Style
    d. Voice

49. In Mr. Booker's first grade classroom, students are studying marine animals in science. Mr. Booker wants to select a book to read to the class that will enhance their understanding of this subject while at the same time capturing their interest in a story. Which of the following would be the best choice?
    a. *The Wild Whale Watch*, part of the Magic School bus series, a chapter book about whales
    b. *The Whale Watchers Guide*, a book designed to help plan a whale-watching trip
    c. *Moby Dick,* a famous 19th century novel about a man and a white whale
    d. *The Pacific Ocean*, a book describing the ocean floor, tides, wave formation, and currents

50. Which of the following describes one difference between role-play writing and early writing?
  a. In role-play writing, the child writes in scribbles that are only meaningful to him or her. In early writing, the child uses real letters
  b. In early writing, the child writes in scribbles that are only meaningful to him or her. In role- play writing, the child writes in groups of words with a period at the end
  c. In role-play writing, the child writes in simple forms of language, usually the way the word sounds. In early writing, the child starts to use sight words and familiar text
  d. In early writing, the child has a sense of audience and a purpose for writing. In role-play writing, the child writes from the point of view of an imaginary character

51. Which of the following is a developmental skill a child should have before beginning to write?
  a. Large muscle control
  b. Ability to speak coherently
  c. Small muscle control
  d. Ability to hold a pencil correctly

52. A child using the prewriting strategy called "free writing" will
  a. Make a list of all ideas connected with the chosen topic
  b. Create a visual map on paper to connect ideas
  c. Ask the questions "Who?," "What?," "When?," and "Where?"
  d. Write thoughts and ideas without stopping to edit them

53. Which of the following is NOT a prewriting strategy?
  a. Brainstorming
  b. Visual mapping of ideas
  c. Asking questions
  d. Organizing writing into paragraphs

54. In the organization stage of writing, the writer
  a. Determines the purpose, thesis, and supporting details of the written work
  b. Brainstorms ideas for items to include in the written work
  c. Submits the writing to a classmate for editing
  d. Writes the introduction and conclusion

55. Maria's topic sentence is "My family prepares for holidays in a big way." Which of the following would be the best supporting detail to follow that sentence?
  a. Holidays are just a waste of everyone's time and money
  b. First, we decide who is going to host the holiday dinner
  c. In my family are me, my brother, my sister, and our parents
  d. Afterwards we all help clean up and then relax

56. Which of the following is true of the introduction to a written piece?
  a. It should be written first
  b. It should be written last
  c. It should reinforce the points made in the piece
  d. It is the least important part of a piece of writing

57. Which of the following is not a method of peer editing?
    a. Pairs of students analyze each others' sentences for variety
    b. Groups of students ask questions of the author to make the writing more clear
    c. Students work together to perform a final edit
    d. Students decide whether another student's essay is good writing or poor writing

58. Which of the following should not be capitalized?
    a. State names
    b. Small words like "of" in titles
    c. Proper names
    d. Main words in titles of written work

59. Elena wrote the following paragraph:
    I believe that everyone should try to care for our planet. The best ways to do
    this are through recycling and using natural energy instead of fossil fuels.
    The supply of fossil fuels such as oil and coal will be used up some day, so we
    should try now to use less. Solar panels can reduce the use of fossil fuels.
    Windmills can be used to make electricity. Hybrid cars also use less fuel. If
    we do not try to be "green," our planet will soon be in trouble from global
    warming and the absence of fossil fuels. What kind of world would that be?
The purpose of Elena's paragraph was
    a. Narration
    b. Entertainment
    c. Persuasion
    d. Description

60. Students should learn to write for a variety of audiences because
    a. Writing everything just for the teacher is boring
    b. Their classmates are also a potential audience
    c. Students are more involved in their writing if the audience varies
    d. Students can make political statements with letters to the editor

61. Which of the following genres takes an opinion and defends it?
    a. Essays
    b. Biographies
    c. Memoirs
    d. Informational texts

62. The final resolution of a fictional plot is called
    a. Exposition
    b. Rising Action
    c. Falling Action
    d. Denouement

63. Assonance means that two or more words
    a. Start with the same sound
    b. End with the same sound
    c. Have the same vowel sound
    d. Sound like an item they portray

64. The basics of writing to a particular audience do NOT include
    a. Precise vocabulary
    b. Correct facts
    c. Figurative language
    d. Illustrations or examples

65. The direct instruction model for teaching students to recognize numbers includes
    a. Showing newly introduced numbers more often than other numbers
    b. Having students count the number of dots and match them to a number
    c. Using manipulatives to count and then write a number
    d. Showing students the different ways a number can be written

66. Which of the following is an example of an ordinal number?
    a. 13
    b. One-half
    c. Second
    d. Ten

67. The property of numbers that states that 1 + 3 is the same as 3 + 1 is called
    a. Associative
    b. Distributive
    c. Inverse
    d. Commutative

68. A number system in which the position of a digit in a number determines its value is called a
    a. Relationship system
    b. Place value system
    c Regrouping system
    d. Tens and hundreds system

69. Paper strips and Cuisenaire rods are manipulatives used to teach
    a. Place value
    b. Fractions
    c. Addition of whole numbers
    d. Percents

70. A decimal can be converted to a percent by
    a. Moving the decimal point two places to the right
    b. Dividing by 100
    c. Doubling the number
    d. Moving the decimal point one place to the left

71. By rewriting 5 times 9 as 9 + 9 +9 + 9 + 9, students will learn
    a. The commutative property of numbers
    b. The relationship between multiplication and addition
    c. The relationship between addition and division
    d. The associative property of numbers

72. Although there are 100 addition facts, if students understand commutativity, they actually need to learn
    a. 95 facts
    b. 75 facts
    c. 65 facts
    d. 55 facts

73. Which of the following is NOT a model that helps students understand subtraction?
    a. Take away
    b. Missing addend
    c. Number line
    d. Adding zero

74. Which of the following is NOT a way to teach young children to recognize patterns?
    a. Count by twos beginning with 5
    b. Comparing geometric shapes
    c. Solving for x in an equation
    d. Analyzing the results of a class survey

75. Geometric figures can be classified by
    a The number of sides
    b. The angles where sides meet
    c. Whether they are polygons or solids
    d. All of the above

76. John drew two triangles on a piece of paper, like this:

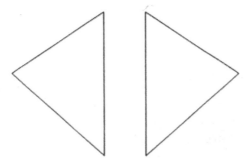

They were facing away from each other, but had the exact same size and shape. This is best described as an example of which geometrical concept?
    a. Rotation
    b. Reflection
    c. Translation
    d. Magnification

77. A missing object problem like the one below is one way of helping students learn what concept?
Truck car bike train truck car bike _____ truck car bike train
    a. Counting
    b. Problem solving
    c. Manipulation of objects

d. Basic addition

78. When deciding to measure the sides of a two-dimensional object, what attributes of that object should be considered?
    a. Volume and liquid measurement
    b. Length and width
    c. Weight and mass
    d. Perimeter and area

79. What is the educational purpose of having students measure the length of an object, such as their desk or table, with non-standard measuring units smaller than the object, such as crayons?
    a. Measuring with small units is easier for young children
    b. Children cannot read the markings on a standard ruler or yard stick
    c. Students learn to measure something larger than a unit with repetitive use of that unit
    d. Students will later be able to transfer measurements from meters to yards

80. For three days, Mr. Hanson had his students keep track of how many times each of them used a pencil during the school day. What is the best kind of graph to use to display these data?
    a. Bar graph
    b. Circle graph
    c. Pictograph
    d. Line graph

81. Katrina wanted to solve this math problem: "If there are 30 days in a month and today is the 12th, how many days until the end of the month?" What should be her first problem-solving step?
    a. Devise a plan for solving the problem
    b. Carry out the plan she created
    c. Look back to check that her answer is correct
    d. Understand what the problem is asking

82. A third-grade teacher decides to introduce new vocabulary words using a word association game. What is required in order for the students to succeed with word associations?
    a. The definition of the new words.
    b. Prior knowledge.
    c. The spelling of the word.
    c. Synonyms of the new words.

83. Which teaching strategy would be best for teaching multiplication tables to a second-grade class?
    a. Priming.
    b. Discussion.
    c. Repetition.
    d. Listening.

84. What is a primary contribution of the Israelites to civilization?
   a. Secularism
   b. Democracy
   c. Monarchism
   d. Monotheism

85. A major scientific development that began near the beginning of the 17th century was
   a. The development of scientific theories
   b. The use of experiments to verify theories
   c. The concept of an attraction between bodies called gravity
   d. The theory of relativity

86. The results of increased production of crops and a managed approach to agriculture is called
   a. The industrial revolution
   b. The information revolution
   c. The agricultural revolution
   d. The scientific revolution

87. Which of these refers to the oceans and water areas of earth?
   a. Atmosphere
   b. Hydrosphere
   c. Exosphere
   d. Lithosphere

88. What is one benefit of a cooperative learning group?
   a. Increased engagement.
   b. Socialization.
   c. Down time for the teacher.
   d. Assistance for struggling students.

89. Due process means
   a. It's important for every citizen to follow the laws of their state and country
   b Any accused person may confront the accuser and provide a defense
   c. Capital punishment is appropriate if a person is convicted of murder
   d. An accused person is considered guilty until proven to be innocent

90. In the Constitution of the United States, which of the following powers are reserved for the states?
   a. Taxation
   b. Declaring war
   c. Regulation of intrastate trade
   d. Granting patents and copyrights

91. A law proposed in Congress but not yet passed is called
   a. A bill
   b. A proposal
   c. An introduced law
   d. A debate

92. It is snack time in your kindergarten class, and you pour two children equal amounts of water; however, one child's cup is bigger. The child with the bigger cup complains that he has less water. In terms of cognitive development, what can you determine by this complaint?
    a. The child has a developmental delay because he does not understand conservation.
    b. The child has not reached the concrete operational stage and does not understand conservation; this is normal for a child of this age.
    c. The child is displaying a delay in intuitive processes commonly acquired during the pre-operational stage of cognitive development.
    d. The child is displaying a preconceptual process that is common among this age group.

93. A belief or opinion in opposition to certain beliefs is called
    a. Respect
    b. Obedience
    c. Dissent
    d. Rights

94. Repetition is important to scientific inquiry because
    a. It is the only way to prove that an experiment is valid
    b. It adds to the number of statistics supporting the concept
    c. It assists the scientist in determining which data to consider
    d. It requires many groups of investigators working on a project

95. The father of microscopy was
    a. Pasteur
    b. Koch
    c. Leeuwenhoek
    d. Watson

96. What effect does science have on technology?
    a. Science verifies what technology discovers
    b. Technology often results from scientific discoveries
    c. Science has no effect on technology; each is independent of the other
    d. Scientific progress is dependent on technology

97. Which of the following are required by all organisms in order to survive?
    a. Water, cells, shelter, and space
    b. Food, water, cellular growth, nurturing
    c. Food, water, sunlight, and air
    d. Air, shelter, space, and companionship

98. What is the difference between mass and weight?
    a. There is no difference; they are the same
    b. Mass is the amount of matter in an object; weight is the pull of gravity on the object
    c. Mass determines the amount of volume of an object; weight does not
    d. Mass is the amount of cubic space that an object occupies. Cubic space is not related to weight

99. World weather patterns are very much influenced by
    a. Wind belts
    b. The Earth's orbit
    c. Ocean currents
    d. Atmospheric conditions

100. In the technological design process, after the problem has been identified and a possible solution selected, what is the next step?
    a. Propose designs
    b. Evaluate the solution
    c. Try out the proposed solution
    d. Report results

101. What steps should precede drawing a conclusion about a hypothesis?
    a. Testing, observing, and recording data
    b. Communicating the hypothesis to others
    c. Comparing data with data of other groups
    d. Writing the results so they can be replicated

Constructed Response

1. Brandon is a five-year-old child who is experiencing typical development in all domains.
   - Describe two developmental characteristics that Brandon is most likely exhibiting.
   - Explain how the characteristics you described are likely to affect Brandon's learning.

2. Part A: A new student and her parents will be coming into your kindergarten classroom before she begins attending your school. List FOUR materials that they would see in a learning center that will promote visual and auditory skills related to reading.

Part B: As the child is exploring the other learning centers of the classroom, how would you explain to the parents how each of these chosen materials will foster a child's visual and auditory skills related to reading based on principles of child development and learning?

3. A first grade teacher plans to read aloud *Frog and Toad Together*, a story by Arnold Lobel. In the story, Frog and Toad struggle with the temptation to eat too many cookies. The passage below describes what happens.

Cookies

Toad baked some cookies. "These cookies smell very good," said Toad. He ate one. "And they taste even better," he said.

Toad ran to Frog's house. "Frog, Frog," cried Toad, "taste these cookies that I have made."

Frog ate one of the cookies. "These are the best cookies I have ever eaten!" said Frog.

Frog and Toad ate many cookies, one after another. "You know," said Frog, with his mouth full, "I think we should stop eating. We will soon be sick."

"You are right," said Toad. "Let us eat one last cookie, and then we will stop."

Frog and Toad ate one last cookie.

There were many cookies left in the bowl.

"Frog," said Toad, "let us eat one very last cookie, and then we will stop."

Frog and Toad ate one very last cookie.

"We must stop eating!" cried Toad as he ate another.

"Yes," said Frog, reaching for a cookie, "we will need will power."

"What is will power?" asked Toad.

- 119 -

"Will power is trying hard *not* to do something that you really want to do." Said Frog.

"You mean like trying *not* to eat all of these cookies?" asked Toad.

"Right," said Frog.

Frog put the cookies in a box.

"There," he said. "Now we will not eat any more cookies."

"But, we can open the box," said Toad.

"That is true," said Frog.

Frog tied some string around the box.

"There," he said. "Now we will not eat any more cookies."

"We can cut the string and open the box," said Toad.

"That is true," said Frog.

Frog got a ladder.

He put the box up on a high shelf.

"There! Now we will not eat any more cookies."

"But, we can climb the ladder, and take the box down from the shelf, and cut the string, and open the box," said Toad.

"That is true," said Frog.

Frog climbed the ladder and took the box down from the shelf.

He cut the string and opened the box.

Frog took the box outside.

He shouted in a loud voice, "HEY BIRDS, HERE ARE COOKIES!"

Birds came from everywhere.

They picked up all the cookies in their beaks and flew away.

"Now we have no more cookies to eat," said Toad sadly. "Not even one."

"Yes," said Frog, "But, we have lots and lots of will power!"

"You may keep it all, Frog," said Toad. "I am going home now to make a cake."

Using your knowledge of first graders' development of literacy and language, answer both of the following:

- Describe two learning activities related to this excerpt that could be used to promote first graders' language and literacy development, making sure to address at least two of the following areas: reading, writing, listening, speaking.
- Explain why each activity you describe would be effective in promoting students' development in the specified areas.

Answers and Explanations

1. D: Analysis. Compare and Contrast is a higher level of thinking and requires analysis.

2. C: Concrete operational stage. The manipulation of objects in the learning process involves using concrete materials to bridge understanding of abstract concepts.

3. B: Conventional. There is actually a hint to this answer in its name. According to Kohlberg, the stage of development during which children learn conventional behavior—e.g., good behavior—is the Conventional Stage.

4. D: Late childhood. This is not one of Erikson's levels of development.

5. B: Microsystem. The family unit and the classroom unit constitute a small social system, a microsystem.

6. C: The importance of play as a learning activity. Vygotsky pointed out that play is the way children learn cooperation and coordination, among other things.

7. A: Students, teachers, and classmates establish knowledge cooperatively every day. In the Constructivist learning theory, the interactions among students, classmates, and teachers were an important contributor to learning.

8. B: The social interaction of students that aid or inhibit learning. According to these theories, students do not just learn in isolation or in a one-on-one relationship with a teacher. They also learn attitudes toward education from their peers, sometimes positive and sometimes negative.

9. C: Report the crisis situation to school or civil authorities. The situation cannot be ignored, but it needs to be dealt with officially and not by the teacher.

10. B: Cooperate with school administrators and public officials to provide assistance, such as a free lunch program and/or academic assistance. Hungry students are not in a position to learn. The family with limited income may not have introduced their child to as many preschool experiences as other children have had, and placement in a special program may be needed to support the child's progress.

11. D: All of the above. There are many possible explanations for a child having decreased attention in class. All should be analyzed to discover the actual problem.

12. B: Acts of jealousy or aggression toward other children. The emotionally-neglected child often behaves negatively toward other children. He or she may not know another way of gaining attention from classmates.

13. B: Play teaches children cooperation and sharing. Play is one way a child learns to relate to other children in a positive way.

14. D: All of the above. Play provides the child with opportunities to develop hand-eye coordination, develop personal interests, and learn to amuse him or herself when alone.

15. D: All areas of development—physical, social, and cognitive—are interrelated. A teacher who is aware of this may be able to emphasize the most appropriate method of instruction for this particular child.

16. D: Developing skills may give clues for the next stage of instruction a student will need. For example, the teacher may observe a child developing skill with manipulative materials and introduce the child to the next step, moving from manipulative to written materials.

17. C: Schizophrenia. The schizophrenic child often has a flat or agitated expression and may speak incoherently or repetitively.

18. D: All of the above. Students with disabilities are best served by a child-centered approach, help in identifying their own learning needs, and need learning experiences that are structured to be appropriate to their needs.

19. B: Sign of emotional difficulties. When children are upset or disturbed, they often manifest their feelings non-verbally in angry outbursts.

20. D: May be abusing drugs. Children using drugs withdraw from social contact and academic activities.

21. B: Having a diagnosed physical or emotional disability that has been professionally evaluated. The child can then be placed in a program that will meet his or her needs. This process often begins with a recommendation by a teacher or parent, but to receive special education services, the child must first be professionally evaluated.

22. A: Lack of sleep or nutrition. Lacking either of these, a child is unable to focus on classroom instruction and may become agitated easily.

23. B: Simile. This phrase is not a metaphor because it uses the word "as" for comparison. A metaphor does omits the words like or as in the comparison. An example of a metaphor would be "He was a frozen statue, motionless beside the door." There is no symbolism in the statement, nor is there any repetition.

24. B: Use in-depth evaluation and early intervention to assist the child with language delays. Research shows that early intervention is highly successful, while a wait-and-see approach just prolongs the delayed language development. Common developmental problems like saying "w" instead of "r" disappear on their own as the child matures and do not need intervention.

25. D: Exaggerated efforts to make friends. The child with emotional problems is likely to withdraw from social interactions and exhibit lower academic performance and aggressive behavior.

26. B: Assign the student an appealing task related to the subject area that requires creativity, research, or in-depth study, such as making a collage or creating a play. Assigning the student to tutor classmates does not assist in the intellectual growth of an academically talented student, and the student is apt to resent such an assignment. The teacher needs to

be aware that academically talented students also have special academic needs and continue to challenge them with meaningful assignments.

27. A: Vary instructional pace and content to meet the specific needs of disabled students. Answers B, C, and D would stigmatize the disabled student and probably not result in a proper pace and content level.

28. D: The students' classroom teacher. Often, disabilities are not apparent in the home setting, and community agencies will not discover disabled children until informed about them, usually by the teacher.

29. B: Parents know their children's needs, and an IEP must be tailored to meet those needs. The classroom teacher will also be aware of some of those needs, but the child spends more time at home than at school, and the parents may be aware of a disability that is not evident in the classroom but needs to be addressed. Also, the implementation of an IEP is most successful when parents, the school, and the community work together as a team.

30. C: Students with disabilities must be educated in an environment appropriate to them and their non-disabled peers, often a regular classroom. Students with disabilities were formerly segregated into special classes, but the least restrictive environment frequently turns out to be a regular classroom, sometimes with additional assistance for the teacher and the student.

31. D: Assisting students in ways beyond what the classroom teacher can provide. This may include any or all of the assistance suggested in the other answers, such as tutoring, counseling, and assisting or advising parents.

32. A: Focuses on helping emotionally or physically disabled students within the classroom. This is the focus of a 504. An IEP has broader applications to other disabilities or special needs.

33. D: The child's behavior is so difficult that the teacher wants the parents to withdraw the child from school. The teacher may desire this, but has no authority to request it from parents. Sometimes a student will attend school for a limited part of the day, but the decision to limit the day or exclude the child will be made by a team, not by the teacher alone in the process of a teacher-parent conference. Conferences are beneficial for sharing information between a teacher and parents and for enlisting parental support for planned activities involving the child.

34. C: These organizations provide opportunities for children to develop leadership skills and learn to appreciate the value of collaborative processes. Not all community resources are directed toward the disabled child. These organizations, ASB and PTSA, are designed to teach leadership skills to students who show leadership potential. Sometimes a student representative is assigned to the school board for the same reasons.

35. A: Alphabet books, wordless picture books, and easy-to-read books. The other genres are more suitable for older children with well-developed reading skills.

36. D: Instruct students in sciences, such as mathematics and biology. Textbooks have that goal. Children's literature is designed to enhance moral values, instruct through entertaining stories, and promote a life-long interest in reading.

37. B: Fantasy. Fantasy stories and books revolve around magical or supernatural creatures. The Harry Potter books are one example of this genre. Science fiction is a similar genre, but relies on the portrayal of a future world, creatures from other planets or galaxies, etc. Action and Adventure involves solving mysteries. Historical fiction stories are set sometime in the past and are usually accurate in their historical information.

38. A: Action and Adventure. One example of this genre is Nancy Drew. Action and Adventure stories do not rely on magical or supernatural events as do Fantasy, Horror, and Ghost stories. They are not biographical unless telling the life of a real person.

39. A: Simile. The statement is not a metaphor because it contains the word "like." A metaphor does not. An example of a metaphor would be "He was a frozen statue, motionless beside the door." There is no symbolism in the statement, "He ran away like a startled rabbit," nor is there any repetition.

40. B: The ability to understand the abstract concept expressed in metaphors is not developed until later in childhood. Analogies are easier for children to understand because they compare known items, whereas metaphors require abstract thinking.

41. C: In addition to plot, character, setting, and theme, a nonfictional work will also introduce interpretations, theories, and research. For example, a biography is a type of nonfiction that may have plot, character, setting, and theme, and in addition it will introduce interpretations and theories (of the person's life and actions) as well as evidence of the author's research.

42. A: How to tell fiction from nonfiction. This is a skill that children learn by following clues within the literature that point out whether the story is true or not. Young children are not yet ready to distinguish bias in an author's writing or understand themes and theories.

43. C: Class composition and preferences. Before selecting literature for the classroom, the teacher needs to assess the class, considering where they are with their reading skills and what their current interests are. After determining these things, the teacher would next evaluate books that seem appropriate for this particular group of children in terms of plot, character, and reading level.

44. D: Provide a wide variety of reading materials for children to choose from. Each classroom will have students who are just beginning to read and some that are reading fluently above grade level. Providing reading materials with an appealing variety of subject matter and broad distribution of reading levels will ensure that every child in the class can select an appropriate book to read.

45. A: Characters. Children enjoy identifying with a character and experiencing life from that character's point of view. If readers do not bond with a character, they will not enjoy the story.

46. D: All of the above. It is not realistic to expect a teacher to preview every book selected for the classroom, and fortunately there are alternatives, such as asking for help from the school librarian, reading professional reviews, and discussing favorite books with children.

47. C: Style. An author writing a humorous book will use a different style than an author writing a biography.

48. B: Point of view. The point of view is generally first or third person. Stories in the second person exist, but these are rare.

49. A: The *Wild Whale Watch*, part of the Magic School bus series, a chapter book about whales. First graders love to listen to chapter books, but most first graders are not quite able to read chapter books on their own. The undersea fictional adventures in this book will impart a great deal of marine information while simultaneously capturing students' attention with the story. The *Whale Watchers Guide* is not a good choice since the class is not planning a whale watching trip. *Moby Dick* is a well-known adult book, which first graders would not understand. *The Pacific Ocean* will probably offer a lot of marine information, but may not capture first graders' interests.

50. A: In role playing writing, the child writes in scribbles that are only meaningful to him or her. In early writing, the child begins to use real letters.

51. C: Small muscle control. Small muscles are those that enable us to make precise motions, such as gripping a pencil and writing letters with it. Large muscle control involves activities such as running or jumping. The ability to speak is not a developmental skill leading to the ability to write.

52. D: Write thoughts and ideas without stopping to edit them. Freewriting is a prewriting strategy that asks the writer to simply write without any internal editing or concern about formalities, such as spelling or punctuation. The purpose of freewriting is to get the flow of ideas going.

53. D: Organizing writing into paragraphs is done either during the writing process or afterwards in the revision stage. It is not a prewriting strategy.

54. A: In the organization stage of writing, the writer determines the purpose, thesis, and supporting details of the written work. In other words, the organization stage is the part of the writing process where the writer decides on the structure of the proposed written work. In this stage, the writer organizes the ideas already decided upon in the prewriting stage.

55. B: "First we decide who is going to host the holiday dinner." A clue is found in the word "first." A list of actions or ideas often follows a topic sentence.

56. B: It should be written last. Although it is the first part of the written piece, the introduction needs to discuss what is in the entire piece. Until the writing is complete, the writer cannot do that. Writing the introduction first runs the risk that what follows may not completely conform to the ideas expressed in the introduction.

57. D: Students decide whether another student's essay is good writing or poor writing. Peer editing should consist of suggestions for improvement and never involve judgmental decisions about quality.

58. B: Small words in titles like "the" and "of." State names, proper names, and main words in titles should all be capitalized.

59. C: Persuasion. Elena's paragraph was written to persuade. Clues to her purpose can be found in the first and last sentences, which clearly try to influence the reader.

60. C: Students are more involved in their writing if the audience varies. Examples of varied audiences include letters to the editor, letters to a friend, an essay written for a community group, and a story written for younger children or beginning readers.

61. A: Essays. In an essay, the writer defends an opinion, giving reasons for that opinion. Biographies are written to narrate the life of a person. Memoirs detail a person's own life and do not defend opinions. Informational texts are factual.

62. D: Denouement. The denouement is the end of the story. The other choices are intermediate steps in writing a story.

63. C: Have the same vowel sound. Words with assonance have the same vowel sound. An example would be cow and loud.

64. B: Correct and accurate facts are not part of the basics of writing to a particular audience. Some writing for some audiences will not be factual at all, for example, a fairy tale written for young children. The basics of writing to a particular audience include precise vocabulary, figurative language, and illustrations or examples.

65. A: Showing newly introduced numbers more often than other numbers. The direct instruction method depends on repetition of newly introduced numbers. Other methods involve counting dots, using manipulatives, and examining different ways of writing a number.

66. C: Second. Ordinal numbers are first, second, third, fourth, etc.

67. D: Commutative. The property that states that the order in which numbers are added does not change the answer is called the commutative property.

68. B: A place value system. That is the system that requires the position of a digit in a number to determine the digit's value. For example, in the number 123, the digit two is in ten's place, and its value is 20.

69. B: Fractions. Students can manipulate the different lengths of materials like paper strips and Cuisenaire rods, in order to determine that one rod is one half the length of the other, for example.

70. A: Moving the decimal point two places to the right. For example, the decimal 3.42 stands for 342.0 percent of something.

71. B: The relationship between multiplication and addition. By performing these activities, students will see that multiplication is just the repetitive addition of a number a certain number of times.

72. D: 55 facts. When students learn that 3 + 8 is 11, they are also learning that 8 + 3 is 11, so they do not need to memorize 100 facts, just 55.

73. D: Adding zero. Adding zero does not assist students in understanding subtraction. Physically taking some objects away from an array of objects, working a problem with a missing addend like 7 + __ = 13 helps students learn that 13-7 = 6. Moving to the left on a number line is another way of helping students understand subtraction.

74. C: Solving for x in an equation. Young children are not ready for algebraic equations, but they can learn to recognize patterns by counting by twos, comparing geometric shapes, and analyzing data they have collected.

75. D: All of the above. Geometric figures can be classified in a number of ways, including the number of sides, the angles where sides meet, and as polygons or solids.

76. B: Reflection. One triangle faces the other. They are alike in all other ways. In a rotation, two like figures are rotated about a central point. A translation is a change in the position of a geometric figure. Magnification refers to a change in size of the figure.

77. B: Problem solving. Because an item is missing in the middle of the pattern, the process asked for cannot be counting or addition. Solving this puzzle does not involve manipulation of objects.

78. B: Length and width. Since the object is not a solid, no other dimensions are needed.

79. C: Students learn to measure something larger than a unit by repetitive use of that unit.

80. A: Bar graph. A bar graph is used to compare quantities. A circle is used to compare parts of a whole. A pictograph shows comparison of quantities using symbols. A line graph shows trends over a period of time.

81. D: Understand what the problem is asking. Before you can solve a problem, you must decide what it is about.

82. B: Word associations require a student to pull from previous knowledge or experience. For example, if the student is presented with the word "aardvark" but has never seen or heard of an   The settlers had not brought enough aardvark, he or she will not be able to make associations. While word association may be a good activity for students after they have reviewed the vocabulary words, it may be counterproductive if the students are unfamiliar with the words. Teachers should also be mindful of cultural differences that may account for a variation in previous knowledge.

83. C: Learning multiplication tables is best accomplished with repetition. As the students repeat the problems and their solutions, connections are made in the brain, and learning is enhanced. While there are many newer methods of teaching and learning, repetition is still useful for a number of tasks. This strategy is also typically used with students learning the

- 128 -

alphabet or their phone number and address. Teachers should be aware that young children have short attention spans and can easily become distracted. Therefore, when using repetition as a teaching strategy, the sessions should be relatively short.

84. D: Monotheism. Before the Israelites, almost all civilizations, including the Egyptian, Greek, and Roman civilizations, believed in many gods.

85. B: The use of experiments to verify theories. Before the idea of experimenting was developed, many scientists had theories, often in conflict with each other, but these ideas were never verified scientifically to demonstrate which one was correct. Experiments provided a way to prove ideas.

86. C: The agricultural revolution. A dependable food supply is essential to all populations. The agricultural revolution, an organized, almost scientific approach to agriculture, increased the food supply necessary for a growing world population.
87. B: Hydrosphere. The earth's environment consists of the atmosphere, (the air we breathe), the hydrosphere (water), and the lithosphere (the land).

88. A: In the classroom setting, some students may be hesitant to openly participate. This may be due to a number of reasons, including the fear of being wrong or shyness. Utilizing cooperative learning groups is one way to increase student participation in class. Creating smaller groups within the class allows students to participate in a less threatening environment. Additionally, motivation and overall outcomes have also been shown to improve in these environments. Using these learning groups in conjunction with other teaching methods keeps students interested and engaged.

89. B: The right of a defendant to confront accusers and to provide a defense.

90. C: Regulate intrastate trade. Intrastate trade is solely within a state, so the state has jurisdiction over it. Taxation is a right granted to both federal and state authorities. Declaring war is a national decision. Patents and copyrights apply to goods made and/or sold throughout the country; therefore, they are a federal responsibility.

91. A: A bill. A bill is a proposed law.

92. B: The child is developing normally; typical of his age group, he is in the preoperational stage of development and has not yet mastered conservation. Conservation is the ability to use logical reasoning to determine quantity. In this case, the child thinks one glass has more water simply because the glass is bigger. As this child enters into the concrete operational stage of development, he will understand that two amounts can be equal despite the size or shape of the container they are in. However, since this skill is not yet developed, the child will continue to believe one has more. If the teacher pours the water from the bigger glass into a glass that equals the size of his classmate's, the child will have a different reaction and possibly think the two are now equal.

93. C: Dissent. Dissent occurs when a citizen disagrees with a certain concept or law.

94. A: It is the only way to prove that an experiment is valid. If an experiment can't be successfully repeated with the same outcome, one cannot determine that the experimental results are valid. Repetition is the key to scientific progress.

95. C: Leeuwenhoek. Pasteur discovered the role of micro-organisms in disease. Koch determined that each disease has a specific pathogen. James Watson developed the science of genetics.

96. B: Technology often results from scientific discoveries. The relationship between science and technology is evident when scientific discoveries prompt technologic advances.

97. C: Food, water, sunlight, and air. All living organisms need food, water, sunlight and air. Shelter, space, and nurturing are nice to have but not crucial to sustaining life.

98. B: Mass. Mass is the amount of matter in an object. Weight is the measure of the pull of gravity on an object.

99. C: Ocean currents. Wind belts, the Earth's orbit, and atmospheric conditions have some effect on weather, but ocean currents have the greatest influence.

100. C: Try out the proposed solution. The first step is to identify a problem and propose a solution. Trying the solution comes next, followed by evaluation and reporting the results.

101. A: Testing, observing, and recording data. Before drawing a conclusion about a hypothesis, one should test and observe it and record data about the test results.

Secret Key #1 - Time is Your Greatest Enemy

Pace Yourself

Wear a watch. At the beginning of the test, check the time (or start a chronometer on your watch to count the minutes), and check the time after every few questions to make sure you are "on schedule."

If you are forced to speed up, do it efficiently. Usually one or more answer choices can be eliminated without too much difficulty. Above all, don't panic. Don't speed up and just begin guessing at random choices. By pacing yourself, and continually monitoring your progress against your watch, you will always know exactly how far ahead or behind you are with your available time. If you find that you are one minute behind on the test, don't skip one question without spending any time on it, just to catch back up. Take 15 fewer seconds on the next four questions, and after four questions you'll have caught back up. Once you catch back up, you can continue working each problem at your normal pace.

Furthermore, don't dwell on the problems that you were rushed on. If a problem was taking up too much time and you made a hurried guess, it must be difficult. The difficult questions are the ones you are most likely to miss anyway, so it isn't a big loss. It is better to end with more time than you need than to run out of time.

Lastly, sometimes it is beneficial to slow down if you are constantly getting ahead of time. You are always more likely to catch a careless mistake by working more slowly than quickly, and among very high-scoring test takers (those who are likely to have lots of time left over), careless errors affect the score more than mastery of material.

Secret Key #2 - Guessing is not Guesswork

You probably know that guessing is a good idea. Unlike other standardized tests, there is no penalty for getting a wrong answer. Even if you have no idea about a question, you still have a 20-25% chance of getting it right.

Most test takers do not understand the impact that proper guessing can have on their score. Unless you score extremely high, guessing will significantly contribute to your final score.

Monkeys Take the Test

What most test takers don't realize is that to insure that 20-25% chance, you have to guess randomly. If you put 20 monkeys in a room to take this test, assuming they answered once per question and behaved themselves, on average they would get 20-25% of the questions correct. Put 20 test takers in the room, and the average will be much lower among guessed questions. Why?

1. The test writers intentionally write deceptive answer choices that "look" right. A test taker has no idea about a question, so he picks the "best looking" answer, which is often wrong. The monkey has no idea what looks good and what doesn't, so it will consistently be right about 20-25% of the time.
2. Test takers will eliminate answer choices from the guessing pool based on a hunch or intuition. Simple but correct answers often get excluded, leaving a 0% chance of being correct. The monkey has no clue, and often gets lucky with the best choice.

This is why the process of elimination endorsed by most test courses is flawed and detrimental to your performance. Test takers don't guess; they make an ignorant stab in the dark that is usually worse than random.

$5 Challenge

Let me introduce one of the most valuable ideas of this course—the $5 challenge:

You only mark your "best guess" if you are willing to bet $5 on it.
You only eliminate choices from guessing if you are willing to bet $5 on it.

Why $5? Five dollars is an amount of money that is small yet not insignificant, and can really add up fast (20 questions could cost you $100). Likewise, each answer choice on one question of the test will have a small impact on your overall score, but it can really add up to a lot of points in the end.

The process of elimination IS valuable. The following shows your chance of guessing it right:

If you eliminate wrong answer choices until only this many remain:	Chance of getting it correct:
1	100%
2	50%
3	33%

However, if you accidentally eliminate the right answer or go on a hunch for an incorrect answer, your chances drop dramatically—to 0%. By guessing among all the answer choices, you are GUARANTEED to have a shot at the right answer.

That's why the $5 test is so valuable. If you give up the advantage and safety of a pure guess, it had better be worth the risk.

What we still haven't covered is how to be sure that whatever guess you make is truly random. Here's the easiest way:

Always pick the first answer choice among those remaining.

Such a technique means that you have decided, **before you see a single test question**, exactly how you are going to guess, and since the order of choices tells you nothing about which one is correct, this guessing technique is perfectly random.

This section is not meant to scare you away from making educated guesses or eliminating choices; you just need to define when a choice is worth eliminating. The $5 test, along with a pre-defined random guessing strategy, is the best way to make sure you reap all of the benefits of guessing.

Secret Key #3 - Practice Smarter, Not Harder

Many test takers delay the test preparation process because they dread the awful amounts of practice time they think necessary to succeed on the test. We have refined an effective method that will take you only a fraction of the time.

There are a number of "obstacles" in the path to success. Among these are answering questions, finishing in time, and mastering test-taking strategies. All must be executed on the day of the test at peak performance, or your score will suffer. The test is a mental marathon that has a large impact on your future.

Just like a marathon runner, it is important to work your way up to the full challenge. So first you just worry about questions, and then time, and finally strategy:

Success Strategy

1. Find a good source for practice tests.
2. If you are willing to make a larger time investment, consider using more than one study guide. Often the different approaches of multiple authors will help you "get" difficult concepts.
3. Take a practice test with no time constraints, with all study helps, "open book." Take your time with questions and focus on applying strategies.
4. Take a practice test with time constraints, with all guides, "open book."
5. Take a final practice test without open material and with time limits.

If you have time to take more practice tests, just repeat step 5. By gradually exposing yourself to the full rigors of the test environment, you will condition your mind to the stress of test day and maximize your success.

Secret Key #4 - Prepare, Don't Procrastinate

Let me state an obvious fact: if you take the test three times, you will probably get three different scores. This is due to the way you feel on test day, the level of preparedness you have, and the version of the test you see. Despite the test writers' claims to the contrary, some versions of the test WILL be easier for you than others.

Since your future depends so much on your score, you should maximize your chances of success. In order to maximize the likelihood of success, you've got to prepare in advance. This means taking practice tests and spending time learning the information and test taking strategies you will need to succeed.

Never go take the actual test as a "practice" test, expecting that you can just take it again if you need to. Take all the practice tests you can on your own, but when you go to take the official test, be prepared, be focused, and do your best the first time!

Secret Key #5 - Test Yourself

Everyone knows that time is money. There is no need to spend too much of your time or too little of your time preparing for the test. You should only spend as much of your precious time preparing as is necessary for you to get the score you need.

Once you have taken a practice test under real conditions of time constraints, then you will know if you are ready for the test or not.

If you have scored extremely high the first time that you take the practice test, then there is not much point in spending countless hours studying. You are already there.

Benchmark your abilities by retaking practice tests and seeing how much you have improved. Once you consistently score high enough to guarantee success, then you are ready.

If you have scored well below where you need, then knuckle down and begin studying in earnest. Check your improvement regularly through the use of practice tests under real conditions. Above all, don't worry, panic, or give up. The key is perseverance!

Then, when you go to take the test, remain confident and remember how well you did on the practice tests. If you can score high enough on a practice test, then you can do the same on the real thing.

General Strategies

The most important thing you can do is to ignore your fears and jump into the test immediately. Do not be overwhelmed by any strange-sounding terms. You have to jump into the test like jumping into a pool—all at once is the easiest way.

Make Predictions

As you read and understand the question, try to guess what the answer will be. Remember that several of the answer choices are wrong, and once you begin reading them, your mind will immediately become cluttered with answer choices designed to throw you off. Your mind is typically the most focused immediately after you have read the question and digested its contents. If you can, try to predict what the correct answer will be. You may be surprised at what you can predict.

Quickly scan the choices and see if your prediction is in the listed answer choices. If it is, then you can be quite confident that you have the right answer. It still won't hurt to check the other answer choices, but most of the time, you've got it!

Answer the Question

It may seem obvious to only pick answer choices that answer the question, but the test writers can create some excellent answer choices that are wrong. Don't pick an answer just because it sounds right, or you believe it to be true. It MUST answer the question. Once you've made your selection, always go back and check it against the question and make sure that you didn't misread the question and that the answer choice does answer the question posed.

Benchmark

After you read the first answer choice, decide if you think it sounds correct or not. If it doesn't, move on to the next answer choice. If it does, mentally mark that answer choice. This doesn't mean that you've definitely selected it as your answer choice, it just means that it's the best you've seen thus far. Go ahead and read the next choice. If the next choice is worse than the one you've already selected, keep going to the next answer choice. If the next choice is better than the choice you've already selected, mentally mark the new answer choice as your best guess.

The first answer choice that you select becomes your standard. Every other answer choice must be benchmarked against that standard. That choice is correct until proven otherwise by another answer choice beating it out. Once you've decided that no other answer choice seems as good, do one final check to ensure that your answer choice answers the question posed.

Valid Information

Don't discount any of the information provided in the question. Every piece of information may be necessary to determine the correct answer. None of the information in the question is there to throw you off (while the answer choices will certainly have information to throw you off). If two seemingly unrelated topics are discussed, don't ignore either. You can be confident there is a relationship, or it wouldn't be included in the question, and you are probably going to have to determine what is that relationship to find the answer.

Avoid "Fact Traps"

Don't get distracted by a choice that is factually true. Your search is for the answer that answers the question. Stay focused and don't fall for an answer that is true but irrelevant. Always go back to the question and make sure you're choosing an answer that actually answers the question and is not just a true statement. An answer can be factually correct, but it MUST answer the question asked. Additionally, two answers can both be seemingly correct, so be sure to read all of the answer choices, and make sure that you get the one that BEST answers the question.

Milk the Question

Some of the questions may throw you completely off. They might deal with a subject you have not been exposed to, or one that you haven't reviewed in years. While your lack of knowledge about the subject will be a hindrance, the question itself can give you many clues that will help you find the correct answer. Read the question carefully and look for clues. Watch particularly for adjectives and nouns describing difficult terms or words that you don't recognize. Regardless of whether you completely understand a word or not, replacing it with a synonym, either provided or one you more familiar with, may help you to understand what the questions are asking. Rather than wracking your mind about specific detailed information concerning a difficult term or word, try to use mental substitutes that are easier to understand.

The Trap of Familiarity

Don't just choose a word because you recognize it. On difficult questions, you may not recognize a number of words in the answer choices. The test writers don't put "make-believe" words on the test, so don't think that just because you only recognize all the words in one answer choice that that answer choice must be correct. If you only recognize words in one answer choice, then focus on that one. Is it correct? Try your best to determine if it is correct. If it is, that's great. If not, eliminate it. Each word and answer choice you eliminate increases your chances of getting the question correct, even if you then have to guess among the unfamiliar choices.

Eliminate Answers

Eliminate choices as soon as you realize they are wrong. But be careful! Make sure you consider all of the possible answer choices. Just because one appears right, doesn't mean that the next one won't be even better! The test writers will usually put more than one good answer choice for every question, so read all of them. Don't worry if you are stuck between two that seem right. By getting down to just two remaining possible choices, your odds are now 50/50. Rather than wasting too much time, play the odds. You are guessing, but guessing wisely because you've been able to knock out some of the answer choices that you know are wrong. If you are eliminating choices and realize that the last answer choice you are left with is also obviously wrong, don't panic. Start over and consider each choice again. There may easily be something that you missed the first time and will realize on the second pass.

Tough Questions

If you are stumped on a problem or it appears too hard or too difficult, don't waste time. Move on! Remember though, if you can quickly check for obviously incorrect answer choices, your chances of guessing correctly are greatly improved. Before you completely give up, at least try to knock out a couple of possible answers. Eliminate what you can and then guess at the remaining answer choices before moving on.

Brainstorm

If you get stuck on a difficult question, spend a few seconds quickly brainstorming. Run through the complete list of possible answer choices. Look at each choice and ask yourself, "Could this answer the question satisfactorily?" Go through each answer choice and consider it independently of the others. By systematically going through all possibilities, you may find something that you would otherwise overlook. Remember though that when you get stuck, it's important to try to keep moving.

Read Carefully

Understand the problem. Read the question and answer choices carefully. Don't miss the question because you misread the terms. You have plenty of time to read each question thoroughly and make sure you understand what is being asked. Yet a happy medium must be attained, so don't waste too much time. You must read carefully, but efficiently.

Face Value

When in doubt, use common sense. Always accept the situation in the problem at face value. Don't read too much into it. These problems will not require you to make huge leaps of logic. The test writers aren't trying to throw you off with a cheap trick. If you have to go beyond creativity and make a leap of logic in order to have an answer choice answer the question, then you should look at the other answer choices. Don't overcomplicate the problem by creating theoretical relationships or explanations that will warp time or space. These are normal problems rooted in reality. It's just that the applicable relationship or explanation may not be readily apparent and you have to figure things out. Use your common sense to interpret anything that isn't clear.

Prefixes

If you're having trouble with a word in the question or answer choices, try dissecting it. Take advantage of every clue that the word might include. Prefixes and suffixes can be a huge help. Usually they allow you to determine a basic meaning. Pre- means before, post- means after, pro - is positive, de- is negative. From these prefixes and suffixes, you can get an idea of the general meaning of the word and try to put it into context. Beware though of any traps. Just because con- is the opposite of pro-, doesn't necessarily mean congress is the opposite of progress!

Hedge Phrases

Watch out for critical hedge phrases, led off with words such as "likely," "may," "can," "sometimes," "often," "almost," "mostly," "usually," "generally," "rarely," and "sometimes." Question writers insert these hedge phrases to cover every possibility. Often an answer choice will be wrong simply because it leaves no room for exception. Unless the situation calls for them, avoid answer choices that have definitive words like "exactly," and "always."

Switchback Words

Stay alert for "switchbacks." These are the words and phrases frequently used to alert you to shifts in thought. The most common switchback word is "but." Others include "although," "however," "nevertheless," "on the other hand," "even though," "while," "in spite of," "despite," and "regardless of."

New Information

Correct answer choices will rarely have completely new information included. Answer choices typically are straightforward reflections of the material asked about and will directly relate to the question. If a new piece of information is included in an answer choice that doesn't even seem to relate to the topic being asked about, then that answer choice is likely incorrect. All of the information needed to answer the question is usually provided for you in the question. You should not have to make guesses that are unsupported or choose answer choices that require unknown information that cannot be reasoned from what is given.

Time Management

On technical questions, don't get lost on the technical terms. Don't spend too much time on any one question. If you don't know what a term means, then odds are you aren't going to get much further since you don't have a dictionary. You should be able to immediately recognize whether or not you know a term. If you don't, work with the other clues that you have—the other answer choices and terms provided—but don't waste too much time trying to figure out a difficult term that you don't know.

Contextual Clues

Look for contextual clues. An answer can be right but not the correct answer. The contextual clues will help you find the answer that is most right and is correct. Understand the context in which a phrase or statement is made. This will help you make important distinctions.

Don't Panic

Panicking will not answer any questions for you; therefore, it isn't helpful. When you first see the question, if your mind goes blank, take a deep breath. Force yourself to mechanically go through the steps of solving the problem using the strategies you've learned.

Pace Yourself

Don't get clock fever. It's easy to be overwhelmed when you're looking at a page full of questions, your mind is full of random thoughts and feeling confused, and the clock is ticking down faster than you would like. Calm down and maintain the pace that you have set for yourself. As long as you are on track by monitoring your pace, you are guaranteed to have enough time for yourself. When you get to the last few minutes of the test, it may seem like you won't have enough time left, but if you only have as many questions as you should have left at that point, then you're right on track!

Answer Selection

The best way to pick an answer choice is to eliminate all of those that are wrong, until only one is left and confirm that is the correct answer. Sometimes though, an answer choice may immediately look right. Be careful! Take a second to make sure that the other choices are not equally obvious. Don't make a hasty mistake. There are only two times that you should stop before checking other answers. First is when you are positive that the answer choice you have selected is correct. Second is when time is almost out and you have to make a quick guess!

Check Your Work

Since you will probably not know every term listed and the answer to every question, it is important that you get credit for the ones that you do know. Don't miss any questions through careless mistakes. If at all possible, try to take a second to look back over your answer selection and make sure you've selected the correct answer choice and haven't made a costly careless mistake (such as marking an answer choice that you didn't mean to mark). The time it takes for this quick double check should more than pay for itself in caught mistakes.

Beware of Directly Quoted Answers

Sometimes an answer choice will repeat word for word a portion of the question or reference section. However, beware of such exact duplication. It may be a trap! More than likely, the correct choice will paraphrase or summarize a point, rather than being exactly the same wording.

Slang

Scientific sounding answers are better than slang ones. An answer choice that begins "To compare the outcomes..." is much more likely to be correct than one that begins "Because some people insisted..."

Extreme Statements

Avoid wild answers that throw out highly controversial ideas that are proclaimed as established fact. An answer choice that states the "process should used in certain situations, if..." is much more likely to be correct than one that states the "process should be discontinued completely." The first is a calm rational statement and doesn't even make a definitive, uncompromising stance, using a hedge word "if" to provide wiggle room, whereas the second choice is a radical idea and far more extreme.

Answer Choice Families

When you have two or more answer choices that are direct opposites or parallels, one of them is usually the correct answer. For instance, if one answer choice states "x increases" and another answer choice states "x decreases" or "y increases," then those two or three answer choices are very similar in construction and fall into the same family of answer choices. A family of answer choices consists of two or three answer choices, very similar in construction, but often with directly opposite meanings. Usually the correct answer choice will be in that family of answer choices. The "odd man out" or answer choice that doesn't seem to fit the parallel construction of the other answer choices is more likely to be incorrect.

Special Report: How to Overcome Test Anxiety

The very nature of tests caters to some level of anxiety, nervousness, or tension, just as we feel for any important event that occurs in our lives. A little bit of anxiety or nervousness can be a good thing. It helps us with motivation, and makes achievement just that much sweeter. However, too much anxiety can be a problem, especially if it hinders our ability to function and perform.

"Test anxiety," is the term that refers to the emotional reactions that some test-takers experience when faced with a test or exam. Having a fear of testing and exams is based upon a rational fear, since the test-taker's performance can shape the course of an academic career. Nevertheless, experiencing excessive fear of examinations will only interfere with the test-taker's ability to perform and chance to be successful.

There are a large variety of causes that can contribute to the development and sensation of test anxiety. These include, but are not limited to, lack of preparation and worrying about issues surrounding the test.

Lack of Preparation

Lack of preparation can be identified by the following behaviors or situations:

Not scheduling enough time to study, and therefore cramming the night before the test or exam
Managing time poorly, to create the sensation that there is not enough time to do everything
Failing to organize the text information in advance, so that the study material consists of the entire text and not simply the pertinent information
Poor overall studying habits

Worrying, on the other hand, can be related to both the test taker, or many other factors around him/her that will be affected by the results of the test. These include worrying about:

Previous performances on similar exams, or exams in general
How friends and other students are achieving
The negative consequences that will result from a poor grade or failure

There are three primary elements to test anxiety. Physical components, which involve the same typical bodily reactions as those to acute anxiety (to be discussed below). Emotional factors have to do with fear or panic. Mental or cognitive issues concerning attention spans and memory abilities.

Physical Signals

There are many different symptoms of test anxiety, and these are not limited to mental and emotional strain. Frequently there are a range of physical signals that will let a test taker know that he/she is suffering from test anxiety. These bodily changes can include the following:

Perspiring
Sweaty palms
Wet, trembling hands
Nausea
Dry mouth
A knot in the stomach
Headache
Faintness
Muscle tension
Aching shoulders, back and neck
Rapid heart beat
Feeling too hot/cold

To recognize the sensation of test anxiety, a test-taker should monitor him/herself for the following sensations:

The physical distress symptoms as listed above
Emotional sensitivity, expressing emotional feelings such as the need to cry or laugh too much, or a sensation of anger or helplessness
A decreased ability to think, causing the test-taker to blank out or have racing thoughts that are hard to organize or control.

Though most students will feel some level of anxiety when faced with a test or exam, the majority can cope with that anxiety and maintain it at a manageable level. However, those who cannot are faced with a very real and very serious condition, which can and should be controlled for the immeasurable benefit of this sufferer.

Naturally, these sensations lead to negative results for the testing experience. The most common effects of test anxiety have to do with nervousness and mental blocking.

Nervousness

Nervousness can appear in several different levels:

The test-taker's difficulty, or even inability to read and understand the questions on the test
The difficulty or inability to organize thoughts to a coherent form
The difficulty or inability to recall key words and concepts relating to the testing questions (especially essays)
The receipt of poor grades on a test, though the test material was well known by the test taker

Conversely, a person may also experience mental blocking, which involves:

Blanking out on test questions
Only remembering the correct answers to the questions when the test has already finished.

Fortunately for test anxiety sufferers, beating these feelings, to a large degree, has to do with proper preparation. When a test taker has a feeling of preparedness, then anxiety will be dramatically lessened.

The first step to resolving anxiety issues is to distinguish which of the two types of anxiety are being suffered. If the anxiety is a direct result of a lack of preparation, this should be considered a normal reaction, and the anxiety level (as opposed to the test results) shouldn't be anything to worry about. However, if, when adequately prepared, the test-taker still panics, blanks out, or seems to overreact, this is not a fully rational reaction. While this can be considered normal too, there are many ways to combat and overcome these effects.

Remember that anxiety cannot be entirely eliminated, however, there are ways to minimize it, to make the anxiety easier to manage. Preparation is one of the best ways to minimize test anxiety. Therefore the following techniques are wise in order to best fight off any anxiety that may want to build.

To begin with, try to avoid cramming before a test, whenever it is possible. By trying to memorize an entire term's worth of information in one day, you'll be shocking your system, and not giving yourself a very good chance to absorb the information. This is an easy path to anxiety, so for those who suffer from test anxiety, cramming should not even be considered an option.

Instead of cramming, work throughout the semester to combine all of the material which is presented throughout the semester, and work on it gradually as the course goes by, making sure to master the main concepts first, leaving minor details for a week or so before the test.

To study for the upcoming exam, be sure to pose questions that may be on the examination, to gauge the ability to answer them by integrating the ideas from your texts, notes and lectures, as well as any supplementary readings.

If it is truly impossible to cover all of the information that was covered in that particular term, concentrate on the most important portions, that can be covered very well. Learn these concepts as best as possible, so that when the test comes, a goal can be made to use these concepts as presentations of your knowledge.

In addition to study habits, changes in attitude are critical to beating a struggle with test anxiety. In fact, an improvement of the perspective over the entire test-taking experience can actually help a test taker to enjoy studying and therefore improve the overall experience. Be certain not to overemphasize the significance of the grade - know that the result of the test is neither a reflection of self worth, nor is it a measure of intelligence; one grade will not predict a person's future success.

To improve an overall testing outlook, the following steps should be tried:

Keeping in mind that the most reasonable expectation for taking a test is to expect to try to demonstrate as much of what you know as you possibly can.
Reminding ourselves that a test is only one test; this is not the only one, and there will be others.
The thought of thinking of oneself in an irrational, all-or-nothing term should be avoided at all costs.
A reward should be designated for after the test, so there's something to look forward to. Whether it be going to a movie, going out to eat, or simply visiting friends, schedule it in advance, and do it no matter what result is expected on the exam.

Test-takers should also keep in mind that the basics are some of the most important things, even beyond anti-anxiety techniques and studying. Never neglect the basic social, emotional and biological needs, in order to try to absorb information. In order to best achieve, these three factors must be held as just as important as the studying itself.

Study Steps

Remember the following important steps for studying:

Maintain healthy nutrition and exercise habits. Continue both your recreational activities and social pass times. These both contribute to your physical and emotional well being.
Be certain to get a good amount of sleep, especially the night before the test, because when you're overtired you are not able to perform to the best of your best ability.
Keep the studying pace to a moderate level by taking breaks when they are needed, and varying the work whenever possible, to keep the mind fresh instead of getting bored. When enough studying has been done that all the material that can be learned has been learned, and the test taker is prepared for the test, stop studying and do something relaxing such as listening to music, watching a movie, or taking a warm bubble bath.

There are also many other techniques to minimize the uneasiness or apprehension that is experienced along with test anxiety before, during, or even after the examination. In fact, there are a great deal of things that can be done to stop anxiety from interfering with lifestyle and performance. Again, remember that anxiety will not be eliminated entirely, and it shouldn't be. Otherwise that "up" feeling for exams would not exist, and most of us depend on that sensation to perform better than usual. However, this anxiety has to be at a level that is manageable.

Of course, as we have just discussed, being prepared for the exam is half the battle right away. Attending all classes, finding out what knowledge will be expected on the exam, and knowing the exam schedules are easy steps to lowering anxiety. Keeping up with work will remove the need to cram, and efficient study habits will eliminate wasted time. Studying should be done in an ideal location for concentration, so that it is simple to become interested in the material and give it complete attention. A method such as SQ3R (Survey, Question, Read, Recite, Review) is a wonderful key to follow to make sure that the study habits are as effective as possible, especially in the case of learning from a textbook. Flashcards are great techniques for memorization. Learning to take good notes will mean that notes will be full of useful information, so that less sifting will need to be done to seek out what is pertinent for studying. Reviewing notes after class and then again on occasion will keep the information fresh in the mind. From notes that have been taken summary sheets and outlines can be made for simpler reviewing.

A study group can also be a very motivational and helpful place to study, as there will be a sharing of ideas, all of the minds can work together, to make sure that everyone understands, and the studying will be made more interesting because it will be a social occasion.

Basically, though, as long as the test-taker remains organized and self confident, with efficient study habits, less time will need to be spent studying, and higher grades will be achieved.

To become self confident, there are many useful steps. The first of these is "self talk." It has been shown through extensive research, that self-talk for students who suffer from test anxiety, should be well monitored, in order to make sure that it contributes to self confidence as opposed to sinking the student. Frequently the self talk of test-anxious students is negative or self-defeating, thinking that everyone else is smarter and faster, that they always mess up, and that if they don't do well, they'll fail the entire course. It is important to decreasing anxiety that awareness is made of self talk. Try writing any negative self thoughts and then disputing them with a positive statement instead. Begin self-encouragement as though it was a friend speaking. Repeat positive statements to help reprogram the mind to believing in successes instead of failures.

Helpful Techniques

Other extremely helpful techniques include:

Self-visualization of doing well and reaching goals
While aiming for an "A" level of understanding, don't try to "overprotect" by setting your expectations lower. This will only convince the mind to stop studying in order to meet the lower expectations.
Don't make comparisons with the results or habits of other students. These are individual factors, and different things work for different people, causing different results.
Strive to become an expert in learning what works well, and what can be done in order to improve. Consider collecting this data in a journal.
Create rewards for after studying instead of doing things before studying that will only turn into avoidance behaviors.
Make a practice of relaxing - by using methods such as progressive relaxation, self-hypnosis, guided imagery, etc - in order to make relaxation an automatic sensation.
Work on creating a state of relaxed concentration so that concentrating will take on the focus of the mind, so that none will be wasted on worrying.
Take good care of the physical self by eating well and getting enough sleep.
Plan in time for exercise and stick to this plan.

Beyond these techniques, there are other methods to be used before, during and after the test that will help the test-taker perform well in addition to overcoming anxiety.

Before the exam comes the academic preparation. This involves establishing a study schedule and beginning at least one week before the actual date of the test. By doing this, the anxiety of not having enough time to study for the test will be automatically eliminated. Moreover, this will make the studying a much more effective experience, ensuring that the learning will be an easier process. This relieves much undue pressure on the test-taker.

Summary sheets, note cards, and flash cards with the main concepts and examples of these main concepts should be prepared in advance of the actual studying time. A topic should never be eliminated from this process. By omitting a topic because it isn't expected to be on the test is only setting up the test-taker for anxiety should it actually appear on the exam. Utilize the course syllabus for laying out the topics that should be studied. Carefully go over the notes that were made in class, paying special attention to any of the issues that the professor took special care to emphasize while lecturing in class. In the textbooks, use the chapter review, or if possible, the chapter tests, to begin your review.

It may even be possible to ask the instructor what information will be covered on the exam, or what the format of the exam will be (for example, multiple choice, essay, free form, true-false). Additionally, see if it is possible to find out how many questions will be on the test. If a review sheet or sample test has been offered by the professor, make good use of it, above anything else, for the preparation for the test. Another great resource for getting to know the examination is reviewing tests from previous semesters. Use these tests to review, and aim to achieve a 100% score on each of the possible topics. With a few exceptions, the goal that you set for yourself is the highest one that you will reach.

Take all of the questions that were assigned as homework, and rework them to any other possible course material. The more problems reworked, the more skill and confidence will form as a result. When forming the solution to a problem, write out each of the steps. Don't simply do head work. By doing as many steps on paper as possible, much clarification and therefore confidence will be formed. Do this with as many homework problems as possible, before checking the answers. By checking the answer after each problem, a reinforcement will exist, that will not be on the exam. Study situations should be as exam-like as possible, to prime the test-taker's system for the experience. By waiting to check the answers at the end, a psychological advantage will be formed, to decrease the stress factor.

Another fantastic reason for not cramming is the avoidance of confusion in concepts, especially when it comes to mathematics. 8-10 hours of study will become one hundred percent more effective if it is spread out over a week or at least several days, instead of doing it all in one sitting. Recognize that the human brain requires time in order to assimilate new material, so frequent breaks and a span of study time over several days will be much more beneficial.

Additionally, don't study right up until the point of the exam. Studying should stop a minimum of one hour before the exam begins. This allows the brain to rest and put things in their proper order. This will also provide the time to become as relaxed as possible when going into the examination room. The test-taker will also have time to eat well and eat sensibly. Know that the brain needs food as much as the rest of the body. With enough food and enough sleep, as well as a relaxed attitude, the body and the mind are primed for success.

Avoid any anxious classmates who are talking about the exam. These students only spread anxiety, and are not worth sharing the anxious sentimentalities.

Before the test also involves creating a positive attitude, so mental preparation should also be a point of concentration. There are many keys to creating a positive attitude. Should fears become rushing in, make a visualization of taking the exam, doing well, and seeing an A written on the paper. Write out a list of affirmations that will bring a feeling of confidence, such as "I am doing well in my English class," "I studied well and know my material," "I enjoy this class." Even if the affirmations aren't believed at first, it sends a positive message to the subconscious which will result in an alteration of the overall belief system, which is the system that creates reality.

If a sensation of panic begins, work with the fear and imagine the very worst! Work through the entire scenario of not passing the test, failing the entire course, and dropping out of school, followed by not getting a job, and pushing a shopping cart through the dark alley where you'll live. This will place things into perspective! Then, practice deep breathing and create a visualization of the opposite situation - achieving an "A" on the exam, passing the entire course, receiving the degree at a graduation ceremony.

On the day of the test, there are many things to be done to ensure the best results, as well as the most calm outlook. The following stages are suggested in order to maximize test-taking potential:

Begin the examination day with a moderate breakfast, and avoid any coffee or beverages with caffeine if the test taker is prone to jitters. Even people who are used to managing caffeine can feel jittery or light-headed when it is taken on a test day. Attempt to do something that is relaxing before the examination begins. As last minute cramming clouds the mastering of overall concepts, it is better to use this time to create a calming outlook.
Be certain to arrive at the test location well in advance, in order to provide time to select a location that is away from doors, windows and other distractions, as well as giving enough time to relax before the test begins.
Keep away from anxiety generating classmates who will upset the sensation of stability and relaxation that is being attempted before the exam.
Should the waiting period before the exam begins cause anxiety, create a self-distraction by reading a light magazine or something else that is relaxing and simple.

During the exam itself, read the entire exam from beginning to end, and find out how much time should be allotted to each individual problem. Once writing the exam, should more time be taken for a problem, it should be abandoned, in order to begin another problem. If there is time at the end, the unfinished problem can always be returned to and completed.

Read the instructions very carefully - twice - so that unpleasant surprises won't follow during or after the exam has ended.

When writing the exam, pretend that the situation is actually simply the completion of homework within a library, or at home. This will assist in forming a relaxed atmosphere, and will allow the brain extra focus for the complex thinking function.

Begin the exam with all of the questions with which the most confidence is felt. This will build the confidence level regarding the entire exam and will begin a quality momentum. This will also create encouragement for trying the problems where uncertainty resides.

Going with the "gut instinct" is always the way to go when solving a problem. Second guessing should be avoided at all costs. Have confidence in the ability to do well.

For essay questions, create an outline in advance that will keep the mind organized and make certain that all of the points are remembered. For multiple choice, read every answer, even if the correct one has been spotted - a better one may exist.

Continue at a pace that is reasonable and not rushed, in order to be able to work carefully. Provide enough time to go over the answers at the end, to check for small errors that can be corrected.

Should a feeling of panic begin, breathe deeply, and think of the feeling of the body releasing sand through its pores. Visualize a calm, peaceful place, and include all of the sights, sounds and sensations of this image. Continue the deep breathing, and take a few minutes to continue this with closed eyes. When all is well again, return to the test.

If a "blanking" occurs for a certain question, skip it and move on to the next question. There will be time to return to the other question later. Get everything done that can be done, first, to guarantee all the grades that can be compiled, and to build all of the confidence possible. Then return to the weaker questions to build the marks from there.

Remember, one's own reality can be created, so as long as the belief is there, success will follow. And remember: anxiety can happen later, right now, there's an exam to be written!

After the examination is complete, whether there is a feeling for a good grade or a bad grade, don't dwell on the exam, and be certain to follow through on the reward that was promised…and enjoy it! Don't dwell on any mistakes that have been made, as there is nothing that can be done at this point anyway.

Additionally, don't begin to study for the next test right away. Do something relaxing for a while, and let the mind relax and prepare itself to begin absorbing information again.

From the results of the exam - both the grade and the entire experience, be certain to learn from what has gone on. Perfect studying habits and work some more on confidence in order to make the next examination experience even better than the last one.

Learn to avoid places where openings occurred for laziness, procrastination and day dreaming.

Use the time between this exam and the next one to better learn to relax, even learning to relax on cue, so that any anxiety can be controlled during the next exam. Learn how to relax the body. Slouch in your chair if that helps. Tighten and then relax all of the different muscle groups, one group at a time, beginning with the feet and then working all the way up to the neck and face. This will ultimately relax the muscles more than they were to begin with. Learn how to breathe deeply and comfortably, and focus on this breathing going in and out as a relaxing thought. With every exhale, repeat the word "relax."

As common as test anxiety is, it is very possible to overcome it. Make yourself one of the test-takers who overcome this frustrating hindrance.